D1458580

Childcare
— *in* —
Rural
Communities

Scotland in Europe

By

Julia Palmer

This study was funded by Grampian
Enterprise, Grampian Regional Council,
Shetland Islands Council and Ross and
Cromarty District Council with the
Highland and Islands Development
Board and Highland Regional Council.

EDINBURGH : HMSO

ABOUT THE AUTHOR

Dr Julia Palmer has researched a range of issues in the Scottish voluntary sector. She is the author of "Employment Training: The Decline of Care?", and the co-author of "Extending Community Care", both published by SCVO in 1990.

SCOTTISH CHILD AND FAMILY ALLIANCE

S·C·A·F·A

CLANN AGUS TEAGHLAICHEAN
AN ALBAINN

55 Albany Street
Edinburgh EH1 3QY
Telephone 031-557 2780

ACKNOWLEDGEMENTS

Many individuals in the statutory and voluntary sectors have given their time in order to provide data and background information for this report. In particular, SCAFA and the author would like to thank: Alex Hamilton (Depute Director of Social Work, Grampian Regional Council); Marjorie Bain (Director of Housing, Shetland Islands Council); and Victoria Fraser (Assistant Development Officer, Development Services Department, Ross & Cromarty District Council). We would also like to thank members of the mother & toddlers groups, playleaders and nursery teachers in the Donside, Buckie & Rathford Lennox areas of Grampian Region; Brae & Ollaberry in Shetland; and Gairloch Parish, West Ross in Highland Region, for distributing questionnaires and all those who spent time completing them. The figures in the report were drawn by Frances Gilbert and the photographs were provided by Nicola Buist, Gillian Munro, Ross & Cromarty District Council, and the Shetland Museum.

SCOTLAND IN EUROPE

Bronwen Cohen

Director, Scottish Child and Family Alliance

Scotland accounts for nearly a third of the total land area in the United Kingdom but only 9% of its population. With an overall population density which is, at 66 persons per square kilometre, by far the lowest in the UK, Scotland's rural areas are extensive whether defined by sparseness of population, settlement patterns, occupation or land use. They are also very varied, ranging from island fishing communities to hill crofting areas and dormitory villages and possess a variety of cultural traditions and languages, including Gaelic, Lallans, and the Norse influenced dialects of the Northern Isles. This alone suggests the importance of rural policy for Scotland. But additional factors are now highlighting its significance.

Firstly, there has been the growing awareness that time has not stood still in rural areas and that, indeed, significant social and economic changes taking place across Europe amount in some respects to what may be described as a revolution in the countryside. What are these changes? The key changes have been identified in a major study of rural change in Europe (focusing on farms and farm households) carried out for the European Commission by the Arkleton Research Trust. The changes are described by the researchers as:

a. The continuing polarisation of agrarian structures (with a) tendency for increasing proportions of our food to come from a decreasing proportion of farms, with consequent 'marginalisation' of small farms;
b. The steady and sizeable decline in agricultural employment, including family employment;
c. The outward migration from many rural areas in the 1950s and 1960s;
d. The stabilisation and even growth of rural population in the 1970s and to some extent the 1980s, with associated features including return migration and in some cases inward migration of 'new rurals' from cities;
e. Relative and even absolute increases in rural manufacturing employment in many rural areas during the 1970s and increases in service sector employment in the 1980's;
f. The continuing redistribution of population within many rural areas into small towns or villages, and away from the open countryside;
g. The marked increase in female participation rates in many, but not all, rural areas.[1]

Secondly, these changes are highlighting the problems which are being experienced by some rural communities. Scenic and cultural riches have sometimes served to hide the very real deprivation which can be found within rural areas. As noted in a report from a seminar held in 1990 on Rural Poverty and Deprivation in Europe[2]:

> "The standard images of poverty and deprivation as portrayed by the media are almost entirely urban. Decaying tenements, derelict factories, vandalised tower blocks are not rural phenomenon."

But very low levels of income are also a rural phenomenon, and the impact of poverty can be enhanced by lack of services. In England a report by Brian McLaughan for the Department of Environment in 1985 shattered the myth of the rural idyll by revealing that one quarter of all households and one in five of the rural population were living in or on the margins of poverty. In Scotland, where average household income is significantly lower than that of England there has perhaps been a greater appreciation that poverty is not just an urban phenomenon. This SCAFA survey conveys the particular problems of rural families with young children 19% of families overall indicated that their household income was £120 or less per week, and this included 29% of families in one of the communities. Over a third of the families (and over half in one of the communities) said their income was £160 or less per week.

Families are very much caught up with the changes which are taking place across Europe's rural areas. The evidence suggests that fertility rates have not dropped in some rural areas to the same extent as urban areas, but nevertheless the decline that has been taking place - in every European Community country with the exception of Ireland, fertility rates are now below replacement level - has led in, a growing number of rural areas, to smaller families and an increasing number of single child families, highlighting the need for services to overcome the isolation of children and families, particularly in some remote areas. In some areas out migration has exacerbated the problems of isolation, in others inmigration by young families has created new demands.

Rural areas have not been immune from some other changes in household structures. There are, for example, an increasing number of one parent families in many areas - in this survey 7% of families overall rising to 14% in one of the communities. In some areas temporary or seasonal male migration means a further considerable number of families suffering from 'the absent father syndrome'. As seen in Appendix 2, in Thesprotia in Greece a significant number of fathers spend more than six months outside the family house, the likelihood of their doing so varying with the number of their children. In Scotland some fishing and oil related jobs require frequent if not as extensive periods away from home. Absent fathers may not be a new development but more traditional structures of household and community support have diminished. Across Europe there is now less support available through the extended family from grandparents, uncles and aunts, and where it exists it frequently cannot adequately meet the needs of families when the mother's employment is outside the farm or croft. At the same time, as noted in the European Childcare Network seminar report[1], rural areas in general and farming in particular have become less 'child-friendly' with increased traffic, mechanisation and growing use of chemicals reducing the opportunity for safe, unsupervised play - and informal community 'supervision' that has been common in some rural areas.

Perhaps the most significant of the changes taking place is the rise in maternal employment rates, involving the increasing visibility of women's work and changing childcare needs with the increase in employment off the farm and croft. This survey confirms the rise in maternal employment rates taking place in many rural areas. In three out of the four communities employment rates for the mothers of under-fives are higher than the 1988 UK average.

For service providers, the substantial and increasing care requirements of rural families bring a further dimension to the existing shortfall in educational services for all pre-school children and in meeting the needs of particular groups in relation to language requirements or the special needs of physically and mentally handicapped children. Throughout Europe the evidence suggests that the level of services is considerably lower in rural than urban areas, prompting the European Commission to prioritise the improvement of services in rural areas under its Third Equal Opportunities Action Programme. Again this survey confirms the considerable shortfall in provision meeting the particular education and care requirements in the study areas. Nursery education and day nurseries both represent strong specific parental preferences whether or not women are in paid employment.

Appendix 2 of this report, together with the SCAFA study illustrate a number of common themes within the provision of rural childcare in Europe. One of these is the search for ways of extending services to sparsely populated and remote areas which has frequently involved an innovative approach in adapting models and sometimes legislation. In Denmark this has involved developing some 'age integrated' centres within schools enhancing in some cases the viability of the schools, and legislative changes to allow the public funding of smaller 'hybrid' nurseries involving family daycare in providing care for up to ten children in one household. In a number of countries too there is a developing interest in 'multi-functionalism' and the possibility of multi-functional centres providing for a variety of local needs of children and women was suggested at the European Childcare Network Seminar on rural areas.

Self-help has been perhaps most explicitly and extensively used in the rural areas of the United Kingdom and Ireland (through the playgroup movement); in many countries parental care requirements are posing problems for services which rely heavily on parents as voluntary workers themselves. In Belgium the ONE Action Research Project involves a wider community self-help model by involving parents as developers and managers assisted by older and younger members of the community within a framework of extensive public support (including paid workers) to replicate what is seen "as a return to traditional rural childcare patterns". The need for properly trained and adequately remunerated childcare workers is widely seen to be as great in rural as in urban areas.

Throughout Europe there is increasing recognition of the relationship of childcare provision to other aspects of rural development. At one level, this relates to the need to give rural children the same opportunities as their urban counterparts - today's children are tomorrow's parents, workforce, and community leaders - as well as the wider recognition of the role of childcare provision in supporting the language, values and identity of communities. More immediately it is seen to be important to reassure parents that a decision to remain within a community is not at the expense of their children's future. In this respect it is instructive to note the finding of the Thesprotia study that 77% of parents thought that living in the villages **was** adversely affecting their children's career.

At another level, it relates to the role of women within the labour force. This may be seen as not only important in contributing to adequate levels of family income (and this has prompted a number of childcare projects within the Europe Commission's Poverty Programme) but it is now also seen as significant in the diversification of traditional economies as increasingly required by structural changes and the Community's agricultural policies within the European Community.

Recognition of the social and economic requirements of childcare services together with more general concerns over the impact of the Single Market upon rural areas have led to the development of some funding possibilities within the European Commission's Structural Funding Programme. The most disadvantaged rural areas within the European Community are included in Objective 1 regions and a further proportion within part of Objective 5b regions. Within Scotland all of the Highlands and Islands and Dumfries and Galloway are included in this latter category. Appendix 3 summarises funding applications in these areas. The concept behind the funding principles are also relevant, however, to many other rural areas.

This study has been prepared for a major conference held in Elgin in 1991 and sponsored by Grampian Regional Council together with the Scottish Office of the Commission of the European Communities. The purpose of the conference was to examine the Scottish experience within the wider European context, and the objective of this study has been to heighten awareness of Scotland's rural childcare needs and encourage debate on policy development in this area. We are grateful for the funding and assistance provided for this study by Grampian Regional Council, Shetland Islands Council and Ross and Cromarty District Council.

(1) Bell, C. Brydon, JM. Fuller, A. McKinnon, N. Spearman, M. "Economic and Social Change in Rural Europe: Participation by Farm Women in the Labour Market and Implications for Social Policy" in European Commission Childcare Network, *Childcare Needs of Rural Families* CEC P1732/90-EN 1990.
(2) "Rural Poverty and Deprivation in Europe: From Analysis to Action" report of the Arkleton Trust Seminar, Tarland, Aberdeenshire, October, 1990 (forthcoming).

CONTENTS

Chapter 1

INTRODUCTION

This research report looks at childcare provision in rural areas, and focuses in particular on four diverse rural communities in the north of Scotland. In addition to describing the special difficulties faced by rural areas, and current childcare provision, the report details the demands for increased childcare facilities to meet the needs of parents, including non-working women and potential women returners.

The four rural areas on which this report focuses are all located in the north of Scotland (Figure 1.1). They are Donside Electoral Division, Buckie & Rathford Lennox Electoral Divisions, both in Grampian Region; the parish of Gairloch, Ross & Cromarty District, Highland Region; and the villages of Ollaberry & Brae in Shetland.

The criteria for defining rural areas are: distance from main services; small population (usually less than 2,000); and a fishing or farming community, rather than an industrial base. Rural life, is often idealised, promoting images of open spaces, close knit communities and a tranquil way of life devoid of poverty and deprivation. Whilst there is clearly an agreeable quality of life for many residents, such an image can present a distorted picture and obscure the need for additional amenities. For example, while there is an apparent abundance of open space, there is often a lack of formal recreational areas where mothers can take their young children to play (Laxton & Bennett, 1988). Rural areas in a number of respects have difficulties in common with inner cities. Both, for example, may experience high levels of unemployment, bad housing and declining public and private services.

During this century, rural communities throughout Scotland have seen a decline in population until the 1970's, when in many areas this trend was reversed. All rural areas have seen a decline in the agricultural work force in recent decades, resulting from increased mechanisation, and the amalgamation and specialisation of many farms. There has also been a similar decline in employment in other primary industries. Agricultural workers and those in related industries make up the majority of rural poor. The development of tourism has a limited impact on creating new employment opportunities, and tends to reinforce the seasonal nature of low pay characteristics of rural economies. The decline in primary sector employment has not been compensated for by the creation of new jobs. The resultant effect being that many rural areas have high rates of unemployment, but this is disguised by the 'enforced' out migration of the economically active population.

The majority of rural areas have experienced the contraction and centralisation of both public and private services due to their declining population base, the high per capita cost of providing services to scattered communities and increasing restraint in public expenditure (Benfield, 1990). Communities have lost schools, shops, surgeries,

Figure 1.1   Four areas surveyed during the Rural Childcare Survey.

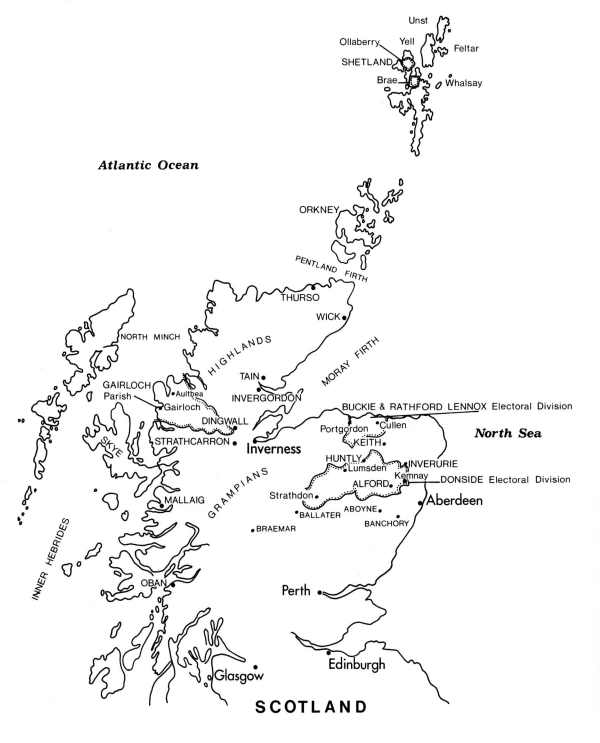

sub-post offices, garages, and telephone boxes. Garages and shops became uncompetitive and lost trade to cheaper filling stations and towns. While many rural residents have managed to cope with the loss of services, a minority have suffered real hardship. The resulting deterioration in the quality of life primarily affects those groups who lack access to transport, and are unable or do not wish to move to larger settlements.

Rural areas usually have above national average levels of car ownership, coupled with a rapid decline in the public transport networks. Lack of mobility affects the most vulnerable groups in communities. They are faced with declining public transport coupled with increasing concentrations of services and amenities in larger centres of population.

The nature of rural deprivation thus derives from a series of interconnected factors. These include the shortage of employment opportunities, the persistence of low pay, the quality and quantity of housing, the decline in public and private services, and the inadequacy of existing transport providing accessibility to services.

FAMILIES IN RURAL AREAS

Recent population changes in some rural areas are the net result of inmigration from urban areas, coupled with the outmigration of the local economically active population in order to seek better housing and employment opportunities. This, in turn, means that the close knit nature of rural communities and extended family networks have been reduced. Incoming families often have no links with the area and do not have local family support to assist with childcare. Local families also can feel isolated through loss of their extended families and through the immigration of others.

CHANGING NEEDS OF WOMEN AND CHILDREN IN RURAL AREAS

Currently provision of care and education services for pre-school children is substantially lower in rural than urban areas. Factors such as dispersed population, transport and fewer available premises contribute to this and the reduction in birth rate has exacerbated the situation in some areas. Despite the lack of statutory and private facilities that are available to provide daycare to pre-school children, economic activity rates of women with dependent children in rural areas are high. They also appear to be increasing in line with national trends.

Changes in rural populations may mean that there are fewer opportunities for working mothers to receive assistance from extended families. With increasing economic activity rates being recorded for all women, grandmothers may be in work and reluctant to give up their own work to become an unpaid childcare provider. There are increasing demands from women for daycare provision to be more widely available in rural areas in order to facilitate their needs to undertake training or return to the labour market.

Children in rural areas also have increasing needs. Falling birth rates mean they are not only less likely to have a sibling, but that there will fewer children of their age group in their community with whom they can play and socialise. Many children are totally isolated. Although playgroups and mother & toddler groups can provide some contact with others, increased daycare facilities would provide them with more opportunities to develop their social skills, learn about their own community, and hence develop stronger sense of community identity.

CHILDCARE AND ECONOMIC DEVELOPMENT IN RURAL AREAS

The increased provision of childcare in rural areas can provide a reverse to rural decline and ageing populations and increase the numbers of younger families with children in the areas. Childcare has now been recognised within the European Commission's Structural Funding Programme (Appendix 3 and SCAFA Fact Sheet No. 5 "European Structural Funds and Childcare") as an issue for economic development. The development of childcare facilities can remove barriers to effective use of the potential labour force; facilitating entry to training in areas of required skills; and encouraging new employers into rural areas.

The increased daycare provision can be significant in offsetting labour market reductions and crucial in encouraging greater numbers of women back into the work force as the demographic dip forecast for the next decade approaches. It can also assist in developing particular skills and addressing the absence of certain skills in the local labour force.

SURVEY AREAS

Although all four of the rural communities surveyed (see Figure 1.1) share many of the same difficulties, they are also very diverse, each community showing a different range of economic, geographic and social problems and have very differing identities.

Gairloch Parish has the lowest population density of the four survey areas (3 per sq. km.) but its population is located along its coast and in valleys, rather than in the mountains inland. The population is traditionally Gaelic speaking, but this has been in decline and is particularly threatened by the high proportion of incoming families to the area. The local economy is based on agriculture and shell fishing, with tourism creating some seasonal employment opportunities.

Donside covers a wide geographic area, and also has a low population density (12 per sq. km.). Its population is located in many very small villages, each with few services, and isolated households. The Donside economy is traditionally based on agriculture, but service industries are also major employers. The area also has a high proportion of incoming families, many of whom work outside the area.

The Buckie & Rathford Lennox area has a high population density (89 per sq. km.) and comprises a series of small towns and large villages along the coast which are traditional fishing communities. In contrast, the small inland population is dispersed in small communities and isolated households, where employment is largely agriculture or forestry related. While the large villages on the coast have a wide range of services and relatively good public transport, the opposite is true of the inland area. In contrast to the other survey areas, Buckie has relatively few incoming families, lower economic activity rates of mothers, and a population which appears to be in gradual decline.

The two villages surveyed in Shetland also contrast with one another. Ollaberry has a dispersed, but stable population, and an economy based on fishing and crofting. In contrast Brae underwent rapid growth in the 70's and 80's, with more than half its population residing in new public sector housing. Employment is mainly either oil or service related, with the Sullom Voe oil terminal and the Brae Junior High School providing opportunities for male and female employment. In contrast to Ollaberry, there is little crofting or fishing related employment.

Chapter 2

GRAMPIAN REGION: BUCKIE & RATHFORD LENNOX, MORAY DISTRICT AND DONSIDE, GORDON DISTRICT.

INTRODUCTION

Two areas were chosen as the focus of this rural childcare research in Grampian Region. The first comprises the Regional Electoral Divisions (EDs) of Buckie (ED 6) and Rathford Lennox (ED 7) in Moray District. The other area is Donside Electoral Division (ED 20) in Gordon District. The population and economic data for these two areas are considered together, but information on local childcare services and demand will be discussed separately.

The Buckie & Rathford Lennox EDs comprise an area of approximately 180 square km. (60 sq. km. of which is covered by forestry) and support a resident population of around 16,000. The majority of this population is centred in the fishing towns and villages along the north coast of Moray District (Figure 2.1). The small communities and scattered farms and crofts inland are accessed by secondary roads and have few local services. Buckie, the largest town in the area, extends 5km. along the coast, but only 1km. inland. The town is surrounded by the villages of Findochty and Portknockie and the town of Cullen to the east, and by Portgordon village to the west. The small town of Fochabers is located 12km. to the southwest of Buckie and on the western edge of the area of study. Fochabers is located on the main A-road to Elgin and represents the only major settlement in the area away from the coast.

Donside ED covers an area of approximately 850 sq. km., including some 60 sq. km. of forestry, and currently has a resident population of around 10,000. Alford, a small town in the centre of Donside, is surrounded by 12 small villages of varying size and many more scattered communities and isolated households (Figure 2.2). The town of Kemnay is located on the northeast boundary of Donside ED. Donside had and still has strong links with the traditional primary industries of agriculture and forestry, and hence until recently has seen a gradual population decline. During the 1970's and 1980's the population increased by 40%, mostly resulting from inmigration. Two A-roads bisect the area and link it to Huntly in the north, Inverurie to the northeast and Aberdeen to the east.

Figure 2.1 Buckie & Rathford Lennox Electoral Divisions, Moray District, Grampian Region.

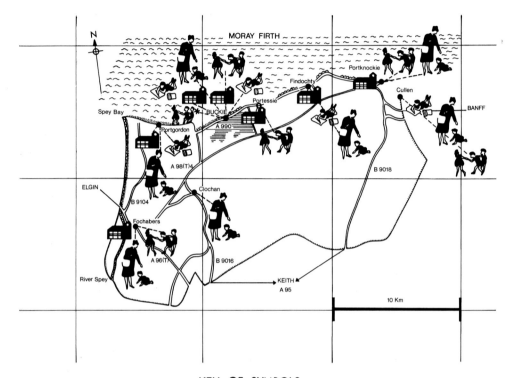

KEY OF SYMBOLS

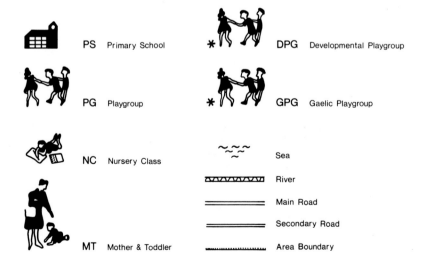

PS	Primary School	DPG	Developmental Playgroup
PG	Playgroup	GPG	Gaelic Playgroup
NC	Nursery Class		Sea
			River
			Main Road
			Secondary Road
MT	Mother & Toddler		Area Boundary

Figure 2.2 Donside Electoral Division, Gordon District and Upper Deeside, Grampian Region.

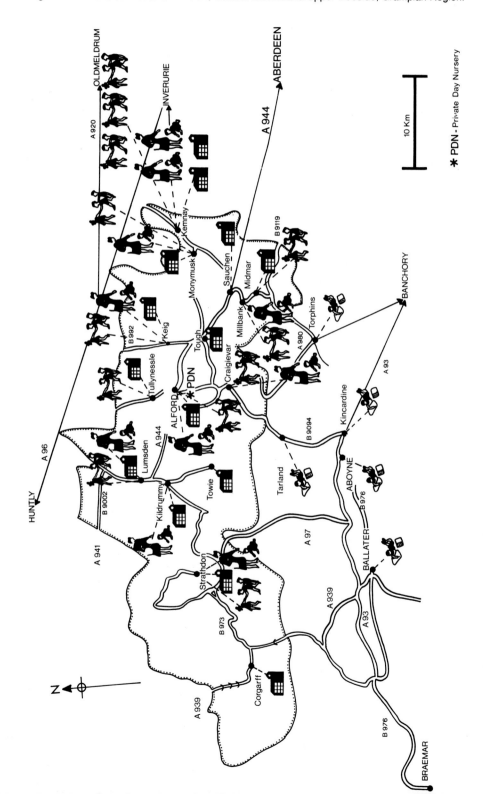

POPULATION AND SETTLEMENT PATTERN

1. *Population*

The distribution of the population within Grampian Region is uneven with a majority of residents now centred within commuting distance of Aberdeen. In contrast most of Grampian's rural areas have suffered from prolonged population decline.

Population in both the Buckie & Rathford Lennox EDs and Donside ED reached a peak towards the end of the 19th century (Table 2.1). In Buckie & Rathford Lennox EDs the population underwent a very gradual decline until 1971 when the trend was reversed, although somewhat modestly. The estimated 1989 population is 3% greater than in 1971, but smaller than that recorded for 1981. These population fluctuations in the Buckie area are related to the prosperity of the fishing industry, which has recently been subject to increased regulation. In Donside ED, rural decline in the 20th century was more marked and continued until 1971. This was related to the decline of traditional rural industries, notably crofting. In the 1970's and 80's the population has undergone continuous growth and is now estimated to be 40% greater than in 1971. Recent growth is almost entirely attributed to migration rather than growth in the indigenous population. The centre and west of Donside ED are both within comfortable commuting distances of Aberdeen and Inverurie.

The age structure of Buckie & Rathford Lennox EDs (Table 2.2) is markedly more elderly than that of either Grampian Region or Scotland. This top heavy effect is commonly seen in areas of prolonged depopulation. Although the decline in the Buckie population was gradual, recent growth has also been modest. Tightening regulations on the fishing industry have probably also resulted in the drift of people, particularly in the 20 - 34 age group away to larger centres of population in search of more secure employment. In contrast the age structure in Donside ED is more youthful and reflects

Table 2.1 - Population Changes in Buckie & Rathford Lennox EDs, Moray District, Donside ED, Gordon District and Grampian Region.							
	1861	1901	1951	1961	1971	1981	1989
Buckie & Rathford Lennox EDs	13,538	18,996	17,612	16,177	15,681	16,264	16,020
Moray District	-	-	-	-	-	64,088	74,460
Donside ED	14,277	14,962	9,744	8,438	7,014	9,072	10,060
Gordon District	-	-	-	-	-	83,896	84,870
Grampian Region	-	-	-	-	-	480,000	*497,450
* 1988 estimate of population for Grampian Region.							
(Source: Census of Population 1861, 1901, 1951, 1961, 1971, 1981 and 1988/89 estimates from Grampian Regional Council).							

both the regional and national average. This has resulted from large increases in people of working age migrating to the area during the 1970's.

Grampian Region estimate that there are currently 1,000 pre-school children in Buckie & Rathford Lennox EDs, with a further 600 pre-school children in Donside ED.

Table 2.2 - 1981 Age Structure of Buckie & Rathford Lennox Electoral Divisions, Donside Electoral Division, Grampian Region and Scotland (%).				
Percentage of Population Aged	Buckie & Rathford Lennox	Donside	Grampian	Scotland
0 - 4	5.9	7.7	6.4	6.2
5 - 15	17.1	19.1	16.5	17.2
16 - 19	6.3	5.4	6.6	7.1
20 - 34	18.5	22.5	22.9	21.8
35 - 49	16.8	16.9	17.4	17.5
50 - 64	17.8	14.1	15.8	16.5
65+	17.6	14.3	14.4	13.7
(Source: Census of Population 1981)				

2. Settlement Pattern and Services in Buckie & Rathford Lennox EDs

The major settlements in Buckie & Rathford Lennox EDs are concentrated on the coast. There are also some small communities and scattered farms and crofts inland (Figure2.1). The area contains approximately 6,000 households with a resident population of around 16,000 (1989 estimates, Grampian Regional Council).

The main population centre is the town of Buckie, which together with Portessie, has 3,300 households and 8,400 residents. The villages of Portgordon (350 households, 760 residents) to the west and Findochty (480 households, 1,020 residents), Portknockie (540 households, 1,220 residents) and Cullen (680 households, 1,410 residents) to the east are linked to Buckie by two major roads. Fochabers, the only major settlement in the area away from the coast comprises some 640 households with 1,520 residents. All housing and population estimates are for 1989, the latest available from Grampian Regional Council.

These major settlements all have a wide range of facilities such as shops, banks and health care that would be expected in small towns or large villages. Each has a primary school and a community centre. Buckie has a high school (school roll 889), and two primary schools (school rolls 356 & 255). Both of these have a full-time nursery department, one catering for 40 and the other for 80 pupils at 5 half day sessions per week. The primary schools at Portgordon (school roll 60) and Findochty (school roll 100) each have a part-time nursery department and share the same nursery team. Each provides for 20 nursery pupils at 5 half day sessions per week. Cullen Primary School (school roll 156) also has a part-time nursery department catering for 20 nursery pupils. Primary schools at Portessie (school roll 153) and Portknockie (school roll 122) have no nursery education provision. Fochabers has a High School (school roll 482), and a primary school (school roll 182), but there is no nursery education provision. All school roll figures are for 1990/91 and were provided by Grampian Regional Council.

3. Settlement Pattern and Services in Donside ED

Kemnay, at the northeast boundary of Donside, is the largest population centre in the electoral division with 2,600 residents and 1,300 households. Kemnay is less than 5 miles from Inverurie and around 12 miles from Aberdeen. The town has two primary schools, with school rolls of 215 and 260, and a community high school (school roll 559).

The remaining 7,400 of Donside's population are widely dispersed (Figure 2.2). Alford, a small town in the centre of the area comprises 460 households and 1,170 residents. There is a primary school (school roll 215), community high school (school roll 450) and many other facilities such as shops, banks, a health centre, swimming pool and a tourist information office. Two villages, Keig and Monymusk, each have more than 200 residents and there are also ten other small villages each with between 40 and 100 residents. The majority of the Donside population, however, reside in smaller communities and isolated households. Although there are two major roads running through Donside, road networks linking the many small communities are generally very poor and often become treacherous or impassable during the winter because of their high terrain. Facilities in these smaller village communities range from nothing, to a village post office shop, with a few having a village hall or community centre. There are also 12 small primary schools in Donside ED in addition to the three larger ones at Alford and Kemnay (see figure 2.2). Cluny, Monymusk and Craigievar have school rolls of between 60 and 70 children, and the other nine primary schools currently cater for between 10 and 26 pupils. None of the schools in Donside provide any nursery education at present, but Grampian Region plans to fund a nursery department at one primary school in Kemnay in 1991/92. Housing and population estimates are for 1989, and school roll figures for 1990 were provided by Grampian Regional Council.

ECONOMY

1. *Economic Background*

Historically Grampian Region has always had strong links and dependence on primary sector industries such as agriculture, crofting and fishing. The decline in these industries throughout the 20th century has recently become more marked with the development of the North Sea oil industry in the 1970's and more recently with the continued effects of European Community policies constraining fish catches and agricultural production. Despite these changes primary sector industries are still important to rural areas within the region.

In contrast, it has been estimated that in 1988, 45,000 people were in oil related employment, roughly equally divided between offshore and onshore employment. Virtually all the onshore workers live in the region, as do approximately a third of offshore workers. The high levels of oil activity have not only affected manufacturing and construction industries, but have also brought increased spending to the service sector, particularly in hotels, entertainment, transport, finance and personal services. Many of Grampian's public sector jobs (eg Regional Offices, local authorities, universities and research institutes) are based in or near Aberdeen. The public sector, however, continues to employ significant proportions of the work force in rural parts of the region.

Forecasts suggest that during the 1990's Grampian's labour force will undergo faster growth than its gradually ageing population (Department of Economic Development & Physical Planning, Grampian Regional Council, 1990). It is also anticipated that fewer school leavers will go directly into the work force. In order to fill the skills gap, women's activity rates are expected to increase significantly during the 1990's.

2. *Employment Structure*

The most recent guide to employment structures available is from the Census of Employment undertaken in September 1984. No details are available at District level, but the results for Grampian Region are tabulated below (Table 2.3).

In line with national trends, the Census of Employment shows that in 1984 the percentage share of female employees in Grampian Region was 41%, the majority of whom were in part-time employment. The 1984 Census of Employment also showed that 27% of those in employment worked part-time. 47% of female employment was part-time, compared with only 8% of male employment.

Details from the 1981 Census of Population indicate that 31% of the work force (employed & self-employed) in Donside ED were female. 45% of women worked part-time compared to only 2% of men. In Buckie & Rathford Lennox EDs 35% of the work force were female, 37% of which worked part-time. Only 2% of the male employment was part-time (Census of Population, 1981).

Table 2.3 - Employment Structure in Grampian Region, 1984 (%).			
	Male	Female	Total
Percentage of employees in:			
Agriculture, Fishing & Fish Farming	4.9	0.9	3.2
Energy and Water Supply	14.2	2.6	9.5
(Total Primary Sector)	(19.1)	(3.5)	(12.7)
Manufacturing Sector	19.5	12.1	16.4
Construction Sector	12.3	1.2	7.7
Service Sector	49.1	83.2	63.2
Total Employees	124,726	88,036	212,762
	59% male	41% female	
(Source: Census of Employment 1984)			

* The Census of Employment is for employees only and thus excludes self-employed people, which comprise a significant part of the work force in this area.
In 1981, data from the Census of Population indicated that 720 people in Donside ED were self-employed.

As a percentage of the economically active population (aged 16+), 24% of males and 8% of females were self-employed. In Buckie & Rathford Lennox EDs there were 788 self-employed people in 1981 (Census of Population 1981). As a percentage of the economically active population the self-employed represented 16% of the male and 5% of the female economically active population (aged 16+). A large proportion of self-employed people work in the 'traditional' primary industries of agriculture and fishing. Although figures are not available, crofting and agriculture would account for many of the self-employed in Donside ED, while fishing would be more significant in Buckie & Rathford Lennox EDs.

3. *Economic Activity*

The economic activity rates of the 16+ population in Buckie & Rathford Lennox EDs and Donside ED are tabulated below (Table 2.4).

Table 2.4 - Economic Activity Rates (of 16+ population) for Buckie & Rathford Lennox EDs and Donside ED (%), 1981.		
Percentage of Economically Active (of 16+ population)	Buckie & Rathford Lennox	Donside
Male	75.3	80.2
Female	35.0	36.1
Total	53.8	58.0
(Source: Census of Population 1981)		

4. Unemployment

The unemployment percentages for Buckie & Rathford Lennox EDs, Moray District, Donside ED, Gordon District and Grampian Region from 1986 to 1990, as recorded and calculated by Grampian Regional Council are tabulated below (Table 2.5).

Table 2.5 - Unemployment Percentage, Buckie & Rathford Lennox EDs, Moray District, Donside ED, Gordon District and Grampian Region, (%) 1986 - 1990.					
Unemployment Percentage	1986	1987	1988	1989	1990
Buckie & Rathford Lennox EDs	10.3	10.2	7.1	5.8	4.0
Moray District	11.0	11.2	8.2	7.0	4.9
Donside ED	6.8	6.8	5.5	4.7	2.7
Gordon District	7.1	6.5	4.7	3.4	2.4
Grampian Region	9.5	9.0	7.0	5.2	3.9

Figures quoted are for July in any given year. (Source: Department of Economic Development & Physical Planning, Grampian Regional Council)

The gradual decreases in unemployment in Buckie & Rathford Lennox EDs, Donside ED, and Grampian Region between 1986 to 1990 are shown graphically below.

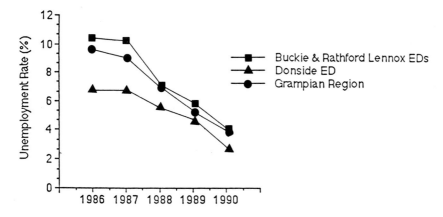

Figure 2.3 - Unemployment rates in Buckie & Rathford Lennox EDs, Donside ED, and Grampian Region, 1986 to 1990.
(Source: Department of Economic Development & Physical Planning, Grampian Regional Council)

Unemployment rates in Buckie & Rathford Lennox EDs in 1986 were higher than the Grampian average, while Donside ED reported lower unemployment. By 1990 the rates for the three areas were converging producing a more uniform picture across the region.

5. *Employment Characteristics of Buckie & Rathford Lennox EDs, Moray District*

Buckie & Rathford Lennox EDs have always had links with the fishing industry. Although this has undergone decline in recent years with constraints on fish catches, the industry is still important to the area. Agriculture and forestry are of more importance on the landward side of Buckie. The public sector is also a major local employer, providing employment at schools, in the health service, etc.

Buckie and its surrounding villages have many opportunities for women to undertake regular full-time or part-time work in schools, shops, hotels, banks and health centres. Employment is also available at a fish factory and two large food manufacturers between Fochabers and Elgin. Despite this, the economic activity rates for women in the area are low, particularly for mothers of pre-school children.

6. *Employment Characteristics of Donside ED, Gordon District*

Donside ED is a traditional rural area with a strong dependence on primary sector industries. Both crofting and farming are of major importance to the area. The local authority also represents a major employer in the service sector providing employment in schools, social services, health, and maintenance workers for roads, water, etc.

In recent years Donside has undergone a significant increase in population, with many of these people working outside the area - some commuting to Inverurie or Aberdeen and others who are offshore workers in the oil industry.

Apart from the schools throughout the area and services based in Alford, there are few local opportunities for women in the rural parts of the area to undertake regular full-time or part-time employment. Those who find employment are not able to rely on public transport, so must have their own transport. Many women with pre-school children find that the cost of petrol and car maintenance costs, together with childcare tend not to make employment economically viable.

CHILDCARE SERVICES

1. *Childcare Services in Buckie & Rathford Lennox EDs*

There is a mixture of statutory and voluntary sector provision for pre-school children throughout the area, but the different types of provision are not equitably available to children in different villages. There are no local authority day nurseries and only 11 registered childminders (6 in and 5 outwith Buckie), but there are nursery education classes attached to several primary schools, each taking children for 5 half-day 2¼ hour) sessions per week. On this basis the primary schools at Portgordon, Findochty and Cullen can each cater for 20 pupils per week, while the two schools in Buckie provide for 80 and 40 pre-school children each week, making a total of 180 nursery places available in the area. The pre-school children in the catchment areas for the schools at Fochabers, Portessie and Portknockie have no access to nursery education.

In contrast the three villages without nursery classes have playgroups, which are absent from all the villages where nursery education is available (Table 2.6). Buckie does have a developmental playgroup for children with special needs. All the villages (except for Portessie) have mother & toddler groups meeting in their community centres or village halls which cater for children aged between 0 and 5. The small community of Clochan also has a mother & toddler group meeting in its community centre. The numbers of places available at different facilities for pre-school children throughout the Buckie & Rathford Lennox area are tabulated below (Table 2.6).

Table 2.6 - Provision of Places for Pre-school Children in Buckie & Rathford Lennox EDs.				
	Nursery Education	Playgroup	Mother & Toddler	Total
Buckie	120	10[1]	80[2]	210
			20[3]	20
			10[4]	10
Clochan	-	-	20	20
Cullen	20	-	35	55
Findochty	20	-	20	20
Fochabers	-	40	15	55
Portessie	-	45	-	45
Portgordon	20	-	25	45
Portknockie	-	30	25	55
1 Teddy Bear Developmental Playgroup for children with special needs				
2 Mother & Toddler Group, Buckie Community Centre				
3 Mother & Toddler Group, Salvation Army, Buckie				
4 Mother & Toddler Group, St. Peter's Chapel, Buckie				

Although there is a total of approximately 535 pre-school places in the area, many pre-school children - particularly those in the 3 to 5 age group - attend more than one type of service. This would mean that substantially fewer than half of the estimated 1000 pre-school children in the area are attending some form of pre-school provision on a regular basis which will bring them into social contact with others of their own age group.

The numbers of pre-school services in Buckie & Rathford Lennox EDs, calculated as full-time equivalents (FTE) per 1,000 of the population aged 0 - 4, are contrasted with those for Grampian Region and Scotland below.

Table 2.7 - FTE Pre-school Places per 1,000 of the population aged 0 - 4 (and per 1,000 of population aged 3 - 4) in Buckie & Rathford Lennox EDs, Grampian Region and Scotland.

	Buckie & Rathford Lennox EDs	Grampian Region[1]	Scotland[1]
FTE places per 1,000 of pop'n aged 0 - 4 (3 - 4) at			
Nursery Education	90 (225)	54 (136)	68 (170)
Local Authority Day Nursery	0	9	16
Childminder	22[2]	42	37
Private Day Nursery	0	—	5
Playgroup	16 (40)	—	—
Mother & Toddler	19	—	—

— Information not available

1 Provisional data for 1989, Scottish Education Department

2 Estimate based on registered childminders (exact numbers of places available are not known)

Table 2.7 shows that the number of FTE nursery education places in Buckie & Rathford Lennox EDs, per 1,000 of the population aged 3 - 4, are greater than those available in Grampian and Scotland. In contrast there are fewer places with registered childminders per 1,000 of the 0 - 4 population, and there are no local authority or private day nurseries.

A selection of the pre-school services are described below:

Buckie Mother and Toddler Group

The Buckie Mother and Toddler Group meets twice a week (one morning and one afternoon) at Buckie Community Centre, where they have the use of the cafeteria area and another large room.

The group is attended by as many as 80 pre-school children, aged from 0-5 and their mothers. Although there are plenty of toys available, there is no structured play nor any segregation into groups of differently aged children.

All the children in their pre-school year also attend one of the morning or afternoon nursery education classes in Buckie, while a minority of three year olds attend the playgroup in the neighbouring village of Portessie.

Mothers at the group did not forsee a need for splitting into a playgroup and mother & toddler group. Those who also want their children to attend playgroup facilities take them to the oversubscribed Portessie group, while others suggested that nursery education should be available for all three year olds.

Teddy Bear Development Group, Buckie

The Teddy Bear Group in Buckie is one of five such groups in Moray District which were set up in 1983. It provides an opportunity for children with special needs in the Buckie area to meet together for two hours twice a week. There are two registered play leaders, two assistants and one student nursery nurse who work with around 10 pre-school children aged between 1 and 4 years. There are no parent helpers at the group, although they are welcome if they wish to stay, and each session costs 50p.

Teddy Bear gives children with physical disabilities or emotional problems an opportunity to meet others of their own age on a regular basis and to receive almost individualised attention from the playleaders and assistants. A minority of these children also attend other pre-school facilities in the area, and in the past many children have graduated from the Teddy Bear Group to integrated nursery education classes. Children with more severe disabilities might stay at the Teddy Bear Group until they are five, before moving on to the special unit at Buckie Community School.

The group also acts as a focus for all the relevant health and education professionals (physiotherapists, speech therapists, occupational therapist and peripatetic teacher for deaf children) who can have the opportunity to meet these children regularly.

Some professionals argue that there should not be segregated provision for children with special needs. However, the general lack of provision for children under five means that for many children with special needs this is the only provision available, particularly for those under three.

The Teddy Bear Group receives grants of 50% of staff costs from the Social Work Department; the Education Department provide the accommodation; and the Health Board provide transport costs (taxis) for the most severely disabled children together with the input of their professional staff. The remaining costs are met from parents' fees and general fundraising.

Mothers outside supermarket, Buckie.

Clochan Mothers & Toddlers Group

The mother & toddler group at Clochan has been in existence for 10 years and meets once a week in a large room at Clochan Community Centre. The centre is a former primary school for children from the community and surrounding farms and crofts, and at a later stage acted as a special school for children with disabilities, but is now used as a community centre by the people of Clochan.

Clochan mother & toddlers is attended by between 15-20 pre-school children aged 0-5, who come not only from Clochan and the surrounding area, but from as far as Buckie, 7 miles away. All the mothers of the children attend the sessions and the charge is 70p per mother.

As the meeting room is spacious, the children usually divide into two smaller groups, one comprising babies and toddlers, and the other comprising older children who are then able to undertake more creative activities such as painting and more active play. The older pre-school children attending Clochan mother & toddlers also attend the Fochabers playgroup 6 miles away.

The group has applied, but received no funding from the Social Work Department. All costs incurred are met by weekly fees and through other fundraising events.

Cullen Mother & Toddler Group

Cullen mother & toddlers meet once a week at the Cullen Community Centre. Approximately 35 pre-school children aged 0-5 attend with their mothers who are charged 50p per week. The group receives no funding from either the Education or Social Work Departments.

Although there is a 20 place nursery education class in Cullen, which "usually has enough places to go around", some mothers would like to see a playgroup set up for at least two mornings a week to cater for 3 and 4 year olds. They are receiving both support and encouragement to make this transition from a local community worker based at Buckie Community High School.

Portgordon Nursery Class

The nursery class at Portgordon Primary School caters for 20 pre-school children five afternoons per week. Portgordon shares its nursery team (nursery teacher and nursery nurse) with Findochty Primary School which offers the same provision to 20 pre-school children in the mornings.

Nursery places are available to children in their pre-school year and occasionally also to those in the preceding year. All places are taken up each year and hence it is not possible to accommodate any pre-school year children who move into the area during the school year.

The nursery class is well stocked with educational toys and materials to provide plenty of opportunities for creative play. In each 2 1/4 hour session, the children undertake a wide range of activities including; painting, cutting and pasting pictures, cooking, eating their snack, washing up, dressing up, etc. The afternoon is completed by a story session.

Nursery classes are free, but parents are asked to contribute one pound per week towards their child's mid-afternoon snack and drink.

Portknockie Playgroup

The Portknockie playgroup is divided into two age groups and meets for a total of five sessions a week. A group of 14 three year olds meet twice a week, while 16 rising 5's (children in their pre-school year) meet three times a week. The group meets in Portknockie village hall and charges 75p per child for each session.

The parents of children using the playgroup are satisfied with the provision, but are aggrieved that there is no nursery education provision available to any pre-school children in Portknockie. They see high quality nursery education provided in the neighbouring villages of Cullen and Findochty at no cost to parents, but in Portknockie parents not only have to pay for, but also organise, the playgroup for children in their pre-school year.

Additional nursery places at Cullen and Findochty are "never available", but even if they were many in Portknockie are unable to drive and so would be unable to take up an option of a nursery education place for their child.

2. Satisfaction with Local Childcare and Demand for New Services

In those areas where nursery education is available, parents of pre-school children are generally satisfied with the provision that is currently available to them. However, as the villages with nursery school classes have no playgroup, many mothers suggested that nursery education should be made more widely available to include all three year olds.

Parents in villages with playgroups, but no nursery education, were less satisfied with the quantity and range of local services available for their pre-school children. All parents expressed the wish for **local** nursery education to be available for **all** children in their pre-school year.

Although many parents were satisfied with the services and other arrangements they were currently using, a substantial proportion would like to see more choice in their own local area. 30% of women in the Buckie & Rathford Lennox EDs would like to have access to a local authority day nursery, and 21% would find temporary creche facilities to be of great benefit. Many women also reported there were too few registered childminders in the area. To fit in with their future plans 14% would like to see the development of an pre- and after-school club five days a week and 23% felt that local holiday play schemes would be of great benefit to them.

3. Childcare Services in Donside ED

In Donside there are no statutory childcare services for pre-school children (ie no nursery education and no local authority day nurseries). There are a total of 21 childminders on the local authority register, not all of whom are currently minding children. They are mostly based in Alford (8) and Kemnay (8), with few in the most rural parts of Donside (Sauchen 3, Monymusk 1, & Tullynessle 1). Until recently registered childminders in Alford ran a self-help support group at Alford community centre, to which they tried to encourage unregistered minders to attend. Unfortunately, they were unsuccessful in motivating others to become registered, and the group no longer meets.

Donside does have a small private daycare facility, based in Alford, which is registered for 15 children and has been providing a service for one year. In addition to playgroups in the towns of Alford and Kemnay, ten of Donside's rural villages and communities have both playgroups and mother & toddler groups. Two playgroups are new developments, starting in March 1991. The local community work team (in Alford) are supportive of these local groups and have been able to provide small start-up grants to all the playgroups.

The community centres in Alford and Kemnay both run temporary creche facilities, but only attached to particular courses that they might be offering, eg a women's group meeting once a week. While this is useful, local women would also like creche facilities to be available that are not tied to specific courses.

Strathdon, Donside.

The numbers of places available at different facilities for pre-school children throughout the Donside area are tabulated below (Table 2.8).

Table 2.8 - Provision of Places for Pre-school Children in Donside ED.			
	Private Day Nursery	Playgroup	Mother & Toddler	Total
Alford	15	51	20	86
Craigievar	-	-	30	30
Keig	-	15	15	30
Kemnay	-	20	20	
		20	20	
		10		90
Kildrummy	-	-	10	10
Lumsden	-	6 *	9	15
Midmar	-	15	-	15
Millbank	-	40	12	52
Monymusk	-	16	8	24
Strathdon	-	13	10	23
Towie	-	11*	-	11
Tullynessle	-	20	20	40

* Projected numbers for new services starting March 1991.

There are approximately 426 pre-school places for children at the private daycare facility, playgroups and mother & toddler groups in Donside. However, many of those pre-school children attending any service often attend more than one, with 3 to 5 year olds attending two or sometimes three different playgroups each week. This means that fewer than half of the estimated 600 pre-school children in the Donside area are attending any form of pre-school provision.

The numbers of pre-school services in Donside ED, calculated as full-time equivalents (FTE) per 1,000 of the population aged 0 - 4, are contrasted with those for Grampian Region and Scotland below.

Table 2.9 shows that there are no nursery education places available for pre-school children in Donside ED unlike the rest of Grampian and Scotland. In contrast there are a greater number of places with registered childminders and at a private day nursery per 1,000 of the 0 - 4 population. There are, however, no local authority day nursery places.

c

Table 2.9 - FTE Pre-school Places per 1,000 of the population aged 0 - 4 (and per 1,000 of population aged 3 - 4) in Donside ED, Grampian Region and Scotland.			
	Donside ED	**Grampian Region**[1]	**Scotland**[1]
FTE places per 1,000 of pop'n aged 0 - 4 (3 - 4) at			
Nursery Education	0 (0)	54 (136)	68 (170)
Local Authority Day Nursery	0	9	16
Childminder	50[2]	42	37
Private Day Nursery	25	—	5
Playgroup	55 (138)	—	
Mother & Toddler	15	—	—
— Information not available			
1 Provisional data for 1989, Scottish Education Department			
2 Estimate based on registered childminders (exact numbers of places available are not known)			

A selection of the pre-school services are described below:

Moira's Little World, Private Daycare Facility, Alford

Moira's Little World is a small private daycare facility, based in Alford. It is registered for up to 15 children and has been providing a service for one year. The service is owned and run by a registered childminder, assisted by one full-time qualified nursery nurse and a part-time assistant who is training to be a nursery nurse. The facility can be used either full-time or part-time by working parents, and is sometimes used on an occasional basis by other parents. Charges are not prohibitive, and vary according to the parents' ability to pay.

The service currently caters for four children full-time, another seven on a regular part-time basis, and acts as a creche facility for other parents. The service is always most busy during school holiday periods, especially the summer, because local playgroups tend not to meet at those times, and there are no playschemes for school children in the area. Many local women consider the service useful as a temporary creche facility, but would not plan to use it as a full-time day nursery.

Lumsden Mother & Toddler Group

Until recently the Lumsden mother and toddler group has been catering for nine children aged between 0 and 5. They have met twice a week in a large, spare classroom at Lumsden Primary School for the last five years. Mothers aimed to undertake creative activities with the six children of playgroup age. This was not always successful and in March 1991 the mothers appointed a playleader to run two sessions per week. One will be for children of playgroup age only, while children of all age groups will attend the other session with their mothers. The previous charges levied of 20p per baby, 50p for older child, and 20p for mothers are expected to rise to around £1.25 per child per session. The initiative for change has come from incoming mothers who have seen playgroups in operation elsewhere. They expect that the development of the playgroup will draw in children from the neighbouring village of Kildrummy (4 miles away), which currently has a mother & toddler, but no playgroup.

During the transitional period, mothers have received support and advice from both the community work team at Alford Community High School, and a local social work assistant who will be involved in registering the group. The playgroup is expecting to receive a start-up grant from the community centre at Alford.

Millbank Community Centre

The Millbank Community Centre is a large former school building, which was recently renovated at great expense (£60,000) by the local authority. It is situated between the villages of Sauchen, Cluny and Tough. The centre is not on a public transport route and anyone wishing to use its facilities must have access to their own transport.

Three different childcare facilities meet in the centre each week: mother & toddler - 12 children once a week; playgroup - 20 children twice a week; and 20 children each at one of the two rising 5's groups each week. Children are able to attend two playgroup sessions per week, and children in their pre-school year may attend one of the two smaller rising 5's groups. The latter are oversubscribed with children coming from as far away as Alford, Keig, Midmar and Craigievar. The charges are 35p per family at the mother & toddler group and £1.25 per child for each playgroup or rising 5's session. The charge for the latter is made whether or not the child attends.

The committee at Millbank comprises both local people and those who have moved into the area. They constantly find themselves under pressure to provide for a greater number of children each week, but continue to limit the numbers at each session so they will be of greater benefit to the children attending them. The lack of facilities in the area for children in the 2 to 3 year old age group also means that many mothers pressurise for their children to be accepted at playgroup at an earlier age.

Parents using the facilities at Millbank consider the building to be an ideal centre for either a permanent or peripatetic nursery project in Donside. Unfortunately the local Education Department is less keen because the nearest primary school at Sauchen is 3½ miles away. However, local primary head teachers would be very supportive of such a project.

Strathdon Playgroup

The Strathdon Playgroup has been in existence for 10 years and meets for two hours once a week at the privately owned Lonach Friendly Hall in the village. There are 13 children on the register who come from a wide area, as far away as Corgarff (8 miles), Towie (5 miles) and Kildrummy (10 miles). This is usually the only opportunity for these children to meet others of their own age group on a regular basis. The charges are £1 per child per session and the playleader is assisted each week by two different parent helpers.

Own transport is essential for parents to bring their children to the playgroup. Until last year one woman used to cycle 8 miles (from beyond Corgarff) to attend playgroup, and she still cycles that distance occasionally to attend her 'local' mother & toddler group at Strathdon.

There are no other daycare facilities or registered childminders in or near Strathdon (the nearest being at Alford, more than 20 miles away). However, four children in the area have been fortunate to be allocated places at the peripatetic nursery education project at Tarland in Upper Deeside. Their parents travel 28 miles (to and from Tarland) with these children twice a week. Although they would prefer more local nursery education, they feel that any provision, even that 14 miles away, is better than none.

4. Satisfaction with Local Childcare and Demand for New Services

In general mothers of pre-school children were satisfied with the actual services that are used by them and their children. However, most stressed that both the quantity and options available to them were very limited and they would prefer a greater amount of childcare facilities in their local areas. This would allow them to make choices rather than just being able to use the only facility in the area.

The fact that there is no nursery education available in the Donside area, is of great concern to parents of pre-school children. 67% of mothers with pre-school children surveyed indicated that they would like to see nursery education available at ideally all, but realistically some, local schools in the Donside area. They felt that a part-time nursery class place should be available for **all** children in their pre-school year.

Other types of new childcare facilities that Donside women would like in their own local area include: a local authority day nursery (38%); creche facilities (6%); while others would like to see increased number of local childminders. To fit in with their future plans 20% would like to see the development of pre- and after-school clubs five days a week and 14% felt that local holiday play schemes would be of great benefit to them.

Figure 3.1   North Mainland, Shetland.

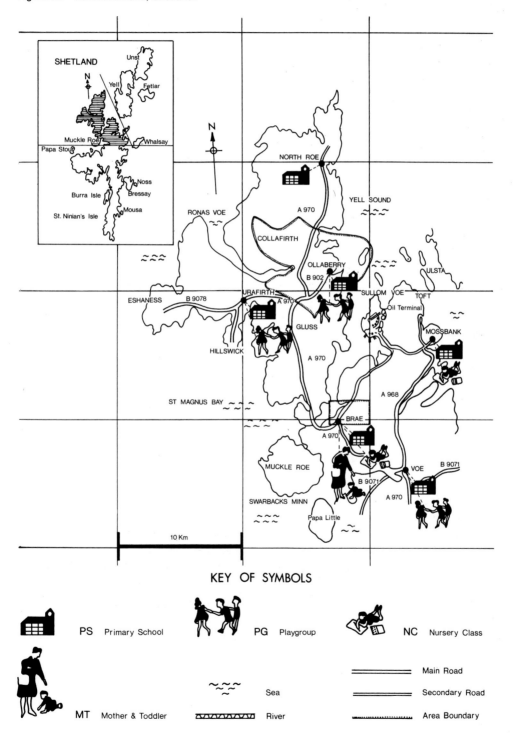

KEY OF SYMBOLS

PS   Primary School   PG   Playgroup   NC   Nursery Class

MT   Mother & Toddler   ~~~   Sea   Main Road

                             River   Secondary Road

                                                      Area Boundary

CHAPTER 3

SHETLAND: OLLABERRY, NORTHMAVINE & BRAE, NORTH DELTING, NORTH MAINLAND

INTRODUCTION

The North Mainland communities of Ollaberry, Northmavine and Brae, North Delting (Figure 3.1) were chosen as the focus of the rural childcare study in Shetland. Both communities were suffering from population decline until the mid-1970's when the development of the oil industry reversed this trend.

The village of Brae comprises an area of less than one square km. and supports a resident population of around 850. The older part of the village with private housing is situated to the south and a public housing estate, built in the mid-1970's, in the east. The rapid population growth during the 1970's was largely due to inmigration rather than any increase in the indigenous population (Shetland Islands Council, 1985). Brae is situated on the main A-road 22 miles north of Lerwick and is around 8 miles from the Sullom Voe oil terminal.

The Ollaberry community is about 11 miles north of Brae village. It covers an area of approximately 22 square km. including the small settlement of Collafirth to the north. The area supports a resident population of approximately 400. Like other areas in the North Mainland, the population decline was reversed during the 1970's, but the growth was more modest than that seen in Brae and Delting (Shetland Islands Council, 1985). Access to both Ollaberry and Collafirth is by a secondary road. Both this road and much of the main A-road to Brae is single track with passing places. Ollaberry is 33 miles north of Lerwick and although geographically close it is approximately 20 miles by road from the Sullom Voe oil terminal.

POPULATION AND SETTLEMENT PATTERN

1. Population

After reaching a peak in the late 19th century, the population of both Northmavine and Delting declined continuously right through until the 1970's. Reasons for this fall in population can be found in the decline of the traditional industries of North Mainland - notably the decline of subsidence crofting and and local fishing industries (Shetland Islands Council, 1985).

The Shetland Islands population increased dramatically from about 1974. This growth can be attributed almost entirely to the effects of the offshore oil developments causing an influx of oil related workers and creating increased employment opportunities for Shetland.

Every local area in Shetland experienced an increase in population during the 1970's and early 1980's (HIDB, 1990). The increase was most marked on the North Mainland, where the population increased by 130% compared with a figure of 34% for the whole of Shetland (Shetland Islands Council, 1985). The North Mainland population growth was entirely due to the impact of oil related developments and the siting of the Sullom Voe oil terminal. These developments have counteracted the previous drift from the rural areas to Lerwick.

Table 3.1 - Population changes in Northmavine, Delting & Nesting and Shetland.							
	1931	1951	1961	1971	1981	1987	1989
Northmavine	1,343	1,054	816	696	748	771	805
Delting & Nesting	1,780	1,426	1,135	1,054	2,755	2,877	2,732
Shetland (total)	21,421	19,352	17,812	17,327	23,130	22,913	23,214

(Source: Census of Population 1931, 1951, 1961, 1971, 1981 & Shetland in Statistics, No.19, 1990).

The growth in the Shetland Islands population over the years has been paralleled by a marked change in the age structure from an elderly to a younger population. In particular the communities of Ollaberry and Brae, on the North Mainland, exhibit significantly high proportions of 0-15 and 20-49 year olds. These age structures are unlike those of most remote rural areas where these is usually a top heavy age structure resulting from prolonged periods of depopulation.

There is an estimated number of 20 pre-school children living dispersed throughout the Ollaberry & Collafirth area (local community worker, personal communication). In contrast Brae village has an estimated 72 pre-school children (Brae Health Centre, personal communication).

Table 3.2 - 1981 Age Structure of Ollaberry & Collafirth, Brae, Shetland and Scotland (%).				
Percentage of Population Aged	Ollaberry & Collafirth	Brae	Shetland	Scotland
0 - 4	9.6	8.8	7.8	6.2
5 - 15	21.1	27.2	17.7	17.2
16 - 19	5.1	6.8	6.2	7.1
20 - 34	28.2	27.2	24.0	21.8
35 - 49	20.8	19.2	17.6	17.5
50 - 64	9.3	8.3	13.0	16.5
65+	5.9	2.5	13.7	13.7

(Source: Census of Population 1981).

2. Settlement Pattern and Services

Much of the population of the traditional communities of Ollaberry & Collafirth are located in or near the lower lying coastal margins. The area contains approximately 70 households, 17 of which comprise the Runnadale public sector estate in Ollaberry.

Facilities in Ollaberry include a shop, post office, public hall, garage, public house, church, and a primary school with a roll of 37 pupils (many of whom live outwith the area of focus). Collafirth has no village shop, hall or church, but does have a small fishing harbour.

Ollaberry has only very limited public transport. There is one bus a day to Lerwick, which arrives at 11am and leaves at 4pm. Such a service would not be suitable for anyone wishing to work in Lerwick.

Brae is the largest village on the North Mainland of Shetland and comprises over 200 households. In addition to the owner occupied accommodation in original Brae village to the south, there are 140 public sector houses on the Moorfield estate and 9 BP rented houses at Gallowburn to the west all built in between 1976 and 1977. The public sector and rented houses are divided by the main road running through Brae village.

Brae has facilities which are utilised by the population throughout the North Mainland, such as the health centre, dental practice and the Junior High School, comprising a secondary department (220 pupils), a primary department (140 pupils) and a nursery education class (catering for 60 pupils at 5 half-day sessions per week). Brae also has a post office, shops, bank, youth centre, village hall, hotel, public house, church, two garages and a swimming pool.

Brae has an infrequent public transport service with a scheduled bus service to Lerwick eight times a day. This service would however enable a resident of Brae to use public transport to commute to Lerwick.

ECONOMY

1. Economic Background

The isolated position of the islands, combined with its relatively small population, poses special problems for the economy of Shetland. In the 1950's and 1960's, restricted employment opportunities meant continued emigration and a steady drain of labour from the islands. The discovery of oil in the North Sea, east of Shetland; the construction of the Sullom Voe Oil Terminal and the development of the related air and marine service industry has done much to reinvigorate the Shetland economy. Concentration of employment opportunities in Lerwick has led to a tendency for both population and business activity to decline in the more distant areas of the region. The traditional industries of fishing, crofting and knitwear do, however, continue to play an important role in the economy, being virtually the only other sectors producing goods for export (HIDB, 1990).

2. *Employment Structure*

The most recent guide to employment structures is from the Census of Employment undertaken in September 1984 and 1987. The results for Shetland are tabulated below.

In line with national trends, the Census of Employment shows the percentage share of female workers is rising, as is the proportion of part-time working. In 1984 40% of all employees in Shetland were female, this had risen to 43% in 1987, the majority of whom were in part-time employment. A Shetland Islands Council Research & Development Department survey showed that in 1983 over 20% of those in employment worked part-time. 47% of female employment was part-time, compared with only 8.5% of male employment.

Details from the 1981 Census of Population indicate 1,425 Shetlanders were self-employed. As a percentage of the economically active population (aged 16+), 16% of males and 5% of females were self-employed. By 1988, information collated by Shetland Islands Council indicates the total of self-employed people had risen to 1,565.

Table 3.3 - Employment Structure in Shetland, 1984, 1987 & 1988.				
	1984*	1987*	1988* (employees)	1988** (self-employed)
Percentage of employees* in:				
Agriculture, Fishing & Fish Farming	2.0	3.0	4.7	44.2
Energy and Water Supply	9.6	8.4	8.7	0.3
(Total Primary Sector)	(11.6)	(11.4)	(13.4)	(44.5)
Manufacturing Sector	13.3	10.7	10.9	8.9
Construction Sector	7.8	7.4	8.7	13.0
Service Sector	67.3	70.5	67.0	33.6
Total Employees*/Self-Employed	9,000	9,139	8,844	1,565
	60% male	57% male	-	-
	40% female	43% female	-	-

(Source: Census of Employment 1984 & 1987; Data for 1988 from Shetland in Statistics, No. 19, 1990).

* The Census of Employment is for employees only and thus excludes the self-employed, which is a significant part of the work force in this area.
** Shetland Islands Council data from 1988 collated employment structures for self employed people.

These data indicate that more than 40% of those self-employed were in the 'traditional' Shetland industries of agriculture and fishing. Knitwear, another traditional industry, accounted for half of the self-employed in the manufacturing sector (5%), while tourism accounted for half of the self-employed people in the service sector (15%).

Table 3.3 does not show the different distributions of the various types of employment throughout Shetland. Data obtained by Shetland Islands Council Research & Development Department in 1983/84 recorded jobs in North Mainland by place of work rather than by employee's place of residence (Shetland Islands Council, 1985).

In Delting 1,691 jobs were recorded, 73% of which were oil-related. Agriculture and fishing accounted for 6% and knitwear for 1% of jobs. 4% of the work force were in the construction sector, while the remaining 16% were involved in providing services.

In contrast, there was no oil-related employment amongst the 334 jobs actually located in Northmavine. 47% of the work force were in agriculture, 16% in fishing or fish processing, with a further 4% in knitwear. The construction sector accounted for 10% of jobs, and the other 23% worked in the service sector.

Table 3.4 - Economic Activity Rates (of 16+ population) for Ollaberry & Collafirth, Brae and Shetland (%), 1981.			
Percentage of Economically Active (of 16+ population)	Ollaberry & Collafirth	Brae	Shetland
Male	81.2	88.4	82.9
Female	27.2	49.6	45.9
Total	56.1	70.5	64.4

(Source: Census of Population 1981)

3. Economic Activity

Employment opportunities, especially in oil-related activities are reflected by high levels of economic activity in the Shetland 16+ population.

4. Unemployment

The unemployment percentages for Shetland from 1981 to 1989, as recorded by the Department of Employment, are consistently lower than the contemporary Scottish figures. However, the fluctuations in the Shetland and Scottish unemployment figures appear to be correlated. The figures are tabulated below (Table 3.5).

Table 3.5 - Unemployment Percentage, Shetland and Scotland, (%) 1973 - 1989.					
Unemployment Percentage	1981	1985	1987	1988	1989
Shetland	5.3	5.5	7.6	6.4	5.8
Scotland	13.5	15.3	13.7	11.3	9.1

Figures quoted are for June in any given year.

(Source: Department of Employment & Shetland in Statistics, No. 19, 1990).

No detailed unemployment figures are available for any area of the North Mainland. However, in 1984 Northmavine's unemployment was slightly higher than the Shetland average, while Delting's was equal to that recorded for Shetland (Shetland Islands Council, 1985).

5. Employment Characteristics of Collafirth & Ollaberry, Northmavine

Ollaberry, in common with other parts of Northmavine, is a traditional crofting community. Many of the men are involved in crofting part-time as well as having secondary jobs. Another important form of employment is the fishing industry which uses the harbour at Collafirth. Other male employment tends to be either Sullom Voe related (e.g. ports & harbours) or manual work with building contractors or with the Shetland Islands Council.

There is little access to regular part-time work in either Ollaberry or Collafirth, which accounts for the significantly low figure for female economic activity. Women tend to be involved in activities, such as crofting or homeworking, which exclude the need to travel. The few job opportunities within the community mean that women in employment would be reliant on access to a car to get the Ronas Voe Fish Factory (4 miles), Brae (11 miles) or Sullom Voe (20 miles). The working hours (6.30am to 3pm) at the fish factory are not convenient for women with pre-school children. These women expressed a wish to work, but not on a full-time basis. However, as all part-time work is outwith the community, it would not be economically viable because of petrol or transport costs in addition to childcare costs (if any). The travelling time would also be too great compared to the time spent actually working.

6. Employment Characteristics of Brae, Delting

Brae is only around 8 miles from the Sullom Voe oil terminal, and over 50% of the male work force in the village is employed either with BP or in oil-related employment (e.g. ports & harbours). Other significant employers are the Junior High School and the two local garages. In common with other parts of Delting, the agriculture and fishing industries do not provide any significant employment for men in Brae.

The are opportunities for both regular full-time or part-time work for women within Brae. The Junior High School generates some full-time opportunities, such as teaching, secretarial and laboratory technical work. There are significantly more part-time opportunities, including kitchen work and playground supervision. The health centre, bank, shops, hotel and public house all generate regular work for women within Brae. There are also opportunities for secretarial and other office work at Sullom Voe oil terminal and BP is currently assessing demand for childcare facilities amongst its local employees.

CHILDCARE SERVICES

1. Ollaberry & Collafirth

There are few childcare facilities for pre-school children in the area. Ollaberry has no day nursery, no registered childminders, no creche, no mother & toddler group and no local nursery education. There is one playgroup and children in their pre-school year are eligible for a place at the nursery education class at Brae Primary (11 miles away).

The Ollaberry playgroup meets for 2 hours once a week in the Ollaberry Public Hall. Although there are two registered playleaders they are not paid for their input. The group also caters for mothers and younger children. The playgroup is registered for up to 18 children (from age 3 to 5) and the average attendance is usually between 15 to 20 children (aged 0 to 5) per session. In addition to the 15 children attending from the Ollaberry and Collafirth area, mothers and children also come from Gluss (3 children) to the south and from as far away as North Roe (4 children), 10 miles north of Ollaberry. The charge is 50p for each child or £1 per child if they use the provided minibuses.

Like all other playgroups in Shetland, the Ollaberry playgroup is able to apply to the

'Ruing' the Sheep, Shetland, 1960's

Leisure and Recreation Department of Shetland Islands Council to fund 50% of their running costs (including rent, heating and lighting costs and also 50% of the play leaders' salary if they are paid). Leisure and Recreation also fund 50% of the transport costs incurred through hiring minibuses. Playgroups are usually successful in applying annually to Leisure and Recreation for 75% grants for new equipment and also receive small annual grants from the Social Work Department.

There is no nursery education at Ollaberry Primary School, but children in their pre-school year are eligible for a place at the nursery education class at Brae Primary (11 miles away). Children are able to and are expected to attend for either 5 morning or afternoon sessions per week, but there is no transport available. Some parents - usually mothers - share journeys, but still find the commitment very demanding. Mothers with no access to a car or those unable to drive find themselves unable to take up the option of a nursery place. Three of the five children in their pre-school year in this area are attending the nursery class. Their parents, who also have children at the Ollaberry Primary School, always have to rely on a friend or neighbour to look after the older child at either the beginning or end of the day while they are en route or returning from the Brae nursery class.

2. Brae

Brae has a nursery education class at Brae Primary School, a mother & toddler group and two registered childminders. There are three other registered childminders in the Firth/Mossbank area 9 miles away which are utilised by some working parents living in Brae. However the village does not have a day nursery, a creche, or a local playgroup.

Children in their pre-school year are eligible for a place at the nursery education class at Brae Primary. The class has one nursery teacher, two nursery assistants and often has the help of a Youth Trainee. The morning and afternoon sessions each last for 2¼ hours and children are able to and are expected to attend for either 5 morning or afternoon sessions per week. Each of the two classes can cater for 30 children, meaning a total of 60 North Mainland children aged between 3 and 5 are receiving nursery education each week. 37 of these children are from Brae village itself, and 3 attend from Ollaberry & Collafirth.

Priority for nursery education is given to:

    i. children with special educational needs as recorded by Educational Psychologists;
    ii. children with special needs as recommended by the Social Work Department;
    iii. children in the year preceding Primary 1 within the catchment area;
    iv. children in the year preceding Primary 1 outwith the catchment area;
    v. children aged three within the catchment area.

Although there is no transport available some parents and children travel from as far as Ollaberry (11 miles), Hillswick (13 miles) and North Roe (16 miles). This is a great commitment from parents because, even if journeys can be shared, there are huge demands on their time and expense. These parents also have to have access to a car, so mothers with no access or who cannot drive are unable to take up the option of a nursery place for their child.

Brae Nursery School, Shetland

The Brae Mother & Toddler Group meets for two hours twice a week in the Brae Youth Centre. The group caters for children aged from 0 to 5 and their mothers. The group is well attended and there are usually 20 or more children per session. The majority of mothers and children are from Brae village and the Moorfield Estate, with two families travelling from outwith the village. There are 30 families who attend regularly, but there are other families with pre-school children in the village who are not on the register. The latter tend to be families with babies or young toddlers. The charge to attend is 60p for the mother and one child or 80p for two children.

Like playgroups in Shetland, the Brae Mother & Toddler Group is able to apply to the Leisure and Recreation Department of Shetland Islands Council to fund 50% of their running costs (including rent, heating and lighting costs) and 75% grants for new equipment. The group could also run a minibus service 50% subsidised by Leisure and Recreation, but have decided against this as the majority of families attending live within walking distance and/or have access to a car.

This mother & toddler group is considering splitting into both a mother & toddler group and a playgroup meeting at the same times on the same days. They would be able to do this as the Brae Youth Centre has two large, warm rooms available. Fieldworkers for the Shetland Pre-School Playgroups Association are supporting and encouraging such a move. This development might also be successful in encouraging mothers with younger babies to attend the mother & toddler group.

3. Satisfaction with Local Childcare and Demand for New Services

65% of the women said they were satisfied the the actual facilities that they and their pre-school children were using. However, the majority of women indicated that they were not satisfied with the range of local facilities from which they were able to choose.

Parents of pre-school children in Ollaberry & Collafirth would like access to nursery education at their local primary school (or at one that is significantly closer than Brae, 11 miles away). While content with the actual service, those parents who currently are using, or plan to use the service, have to travel great distances with their children in order to do so. These parents suggested that the Education Department's insistence that pre-school children attend the nursery class '5 days a week or not at all' was inflexible. This demand is too great a commitment for some parents, in both time and expense, and meant that some children from far-flung villages were being unfairly excluded. Women in Ollaberry expressed a loyalty to their local playgroup and expressed the need for children in their pre-school year to have the opportunity to continue meeting and socialising with children with whom they will attend their own local primary school. Parents living in villages outwith Brae, especially those from as far away as Ollaberry, expressed the desire for some sort of transport service to be available for children attending nursery education. Suggestions included:–

"**if one journey could be tied in with children attending the Brae High School, the burden on parents would be greatly reduced.**" Mother, Ollaberry.

"**A nursery school should be provided in the area in which I live, there are three primary schools within a 4 mile radius, none have nursery provision. The nearest one is in Brae which is 15 miles away. I take my** children to it because I think they need to get out and meet other children of their own age. **If a school provided a nursery up here in the Northmavine district many more children would benefit.**"   Mother, Ollaberry.

Parents in Brae were extremely satisfied with the nursery education that is available to both children in their pre-school year and currently also to many three year olds. 37 of the estimated 72 pre-school children in Brae village are receiving five half-days of nursery education per week.

Excluding the demand for local nursery education in Ollaberry, overall the women from Brae and Ollaberry said the two new services they would most like to see would be a creche and registered childminders in their area. Many women suggested that a creche, available for one or two days per week, would be extremely useful and would enable them to undertake a shopping trip to Lerwick by car, or public transport, without their pre-school children. 50% of the working mothers said they would like to have the use of a workplace nursery and a further 30% said a local authority day nursery.

To fit in with their future plans 19% of women surveyed in North Mainland, Shetland said that they would like to see the development of a holiday care scheme in the area, and 15% would like pre- and after-school clubs to be available.

Chapter 4

HIGHLAND REGION: GAIRLOCH AREA, WEST ROSS

INTRODUCTION

Gairloch Parish (District Ward 3) is one of the most westerly parts of West Ross in the Ross and Cromarty District of Highland Region (Figure 4.1). Its 850 square km supported a resident population of around 2,200 in 1989.

The mountainous landscape, penetrated by deep sea lochs, constrains internal communications and limits agriculture to a largely marginal activity. These features, however, are the basis of the healthy tourism growth which the area has experienced.

POPULATION AND SETTLEMENT PATTERN

1. Population

The distribution of the population in Ross and Cromarty is uneven, ranging from the remote and sparsely populated west coast to the larger towns and villages in the east.

The population of Ross and Cromarty was at a peak in the late 19th century. The population then declined continuously until the late 1960's and 1970's when the trend was reversed due to rapid industrialisation throughout East Ross and at Kishorn in West Ross (HIDB, 1990). Although the Kishorn development was outwith Gairloch Parish, and around 30 miles from Gairloch village, its influence extended as far north as Gairloch and Poolewe (HIDB, 1983).

Table 4.1 - Population changes in Gairloch Parish and West Ross.								
	1861	1901	1951	1961	1971	1981	1985	1988	1989
Gairloch	6,440	3,797	1,991	1,788	1,782	1,934	2,049	2,171	2,194
West Ross	14,447	10,061	4,996	4,545	4,491	4,979	-	6,266	-
Ross & Cromarty	-	43,572	33,708	34,744	34,858	44,872	-	48,202	50,960
(Source: Census of Population 1861, 1901, 1951, 1961, 1971, 1981 & estimates from Highland Regional Council).								

Since 1971 the population of Gairloch Parish has gradually increased and is estimated to have grown by more than 20% by 1989. This has resulted from both growth of the indigenous population and migration from a wider area. There is also some evidence of people retiring to the area.

Figure 4.1   Gairloch Parish, Ross and Cromarty District, Highland Region.

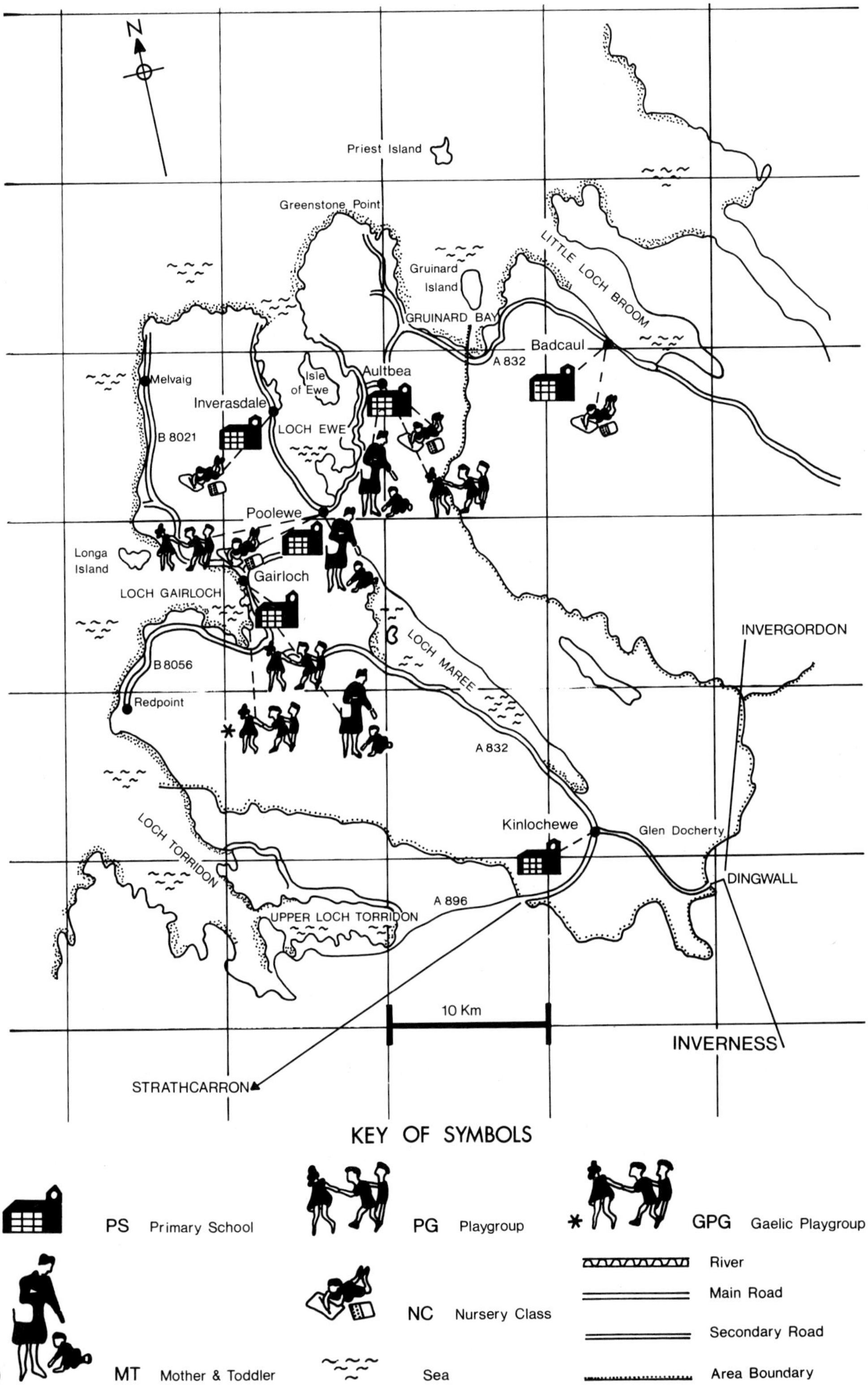

N

Priest Island

Greenstone Point

Gruinard
Island

GRUINARD BAY

Little Loch Broom

Badcaul

A 832

Melvaig

Inverasdale

Isle
of Ewe

Aultbea

B 8021

LOCH EWE

Poolewe

Longa
Island

LOCH GAIRLOCH

Gairloch

INVERGORDON

B 8056

Redpoint

LOCH MAREE

A 832

LOCH TORRIDON

Kinlochewe

Glen Docherty

DINGWALL

UPPER LOCH TORRIDON

A 896

10 Km

INVERNESS

STRATHCARRON

KEY OF SYMBOLS

PS Primary School	PG Playgroup	* GPG Gaelic Playgroup
		River
		Main Road
	NC Nursery Class	Secondary Road
MT Mother & Toddler	Sea	Area Boundary

40

Gairloch Parish, in common with other remote rural areas which have suffered prolonged periods of depopulation, has a top heavy age structure. The Gairloch population structure in 1981 was similar to that for Highland Region, but is significantly more elderly than the average age structures for Ross & Cromarty and Scotland. In 1981 Gairloch Parish had a particularly high proportion of residents over the age of 65, with a comparative shortage of young people in the 16 to 34 age group.

Table 4.2 - 1981 Age Structure of Gairloch, West Ross, Ross & Cromarty, Highland Region and Scotland (%).					
Percentage of Population Aged	Gairloch	West Ross	Ross & Cromarty	Highland Region	Scotland
0 - 4	6.9	6.8	8.1	7.0	6.2
5 - 15	17.1	17.0	19.1	17.6	17.2
16 - 19	4.3	5.4	6.5	6.8	7.1
20 - 34	18.2	18.9	21.6	21.2	21.8
35 - 49	16.8	17.3	17.5	17.6	17.5
50 - 64	17.8	17.3	14.6	15.7	16.5
65+	18.9	17.3	12.5	14.1	13.7
(Source: Census of Population 1981).					

There are currently 130 pre-school children in the Gairloch Electoral District (personal communication local primary schools and health visitors).

Settlement Pattern and Services

The settlement pattern is limited by the mountainous terrain in the landward area which restricts development to the lower lying coastal margins and broad valleys (Figure 4.1). The area contains approximately 1,100 households, of which only 106 are in the public sector (estimates Highland Regional Council, 1989).

The main population centre is Gairloch with an approximate population of 1,025 residents in 567 households. Three secondary centres at Poolewe (228 residents, 101 households), Inverasdale (188 residents, 92 households), and Aultbea (611 residents, 289 households), see Figure 4.1. All three of these villages are located on the coast. Poolewe and Aultbea are connected to Gairloch by the undulating, windy A-road, while Inverasdale is linked to Poolewe by a narrow secondary road with passing places. Another secondary population centre is situated inland at Kinlochewe (142 residents, 289 households). All population and household estimates are from Highland Regional Council, 1989.

Facilities in Gairloch include a bank, branch library, local authority home for elderly people, doctor's surgery, dental practice, community centre, post office, shops, hotels, a primary and secondary school (98 and 170 pupils respectively in 1990/91, Highland Regional Council). There is a Gaelic unit attached to the schools which opened in 1990. Gairloch also has a tourist information centre, heritage museum and a nine-hole golf course.

There are also primary schools in each of the settlements of Aultbea (1990/91 school roll of 59), Inverasdale (school roll 26), Kinlochewe (school roll 23) and Poolewe (school roll 23). All these primary schools feed into Gairloch High School. Aultbea has a village hall, doctor's surgery and a private nursing/old people's home which is due to open in May 1991. Poolewe has a village hall and a swimming pool.

The entire Gairloch area has only very limited public transport. There is only one bus a day to Inverness with a journey time of 3 hours. Such a service would not be suitable for anyone wishing to either work in Inverness or take advantage of further education facilities

Families at work: in the fields, Ross and Cromarty, 1900s.

ECONOMY

1. Economic Background

Twenty-five years ago Ross and Cromarty had an economy based principally on agriculture. Industrial developments in the late 1960's and 1970's, mainly in East Ross but also at Kishorn in West Ross, transformed the economy to one more dependent on manufacturing. However, fluctuations in the oil industry, the closure of the Invergordon aluminium smelter in 1981 and closure of the fabrication yard at Kishorn, West Ross in 1986, have inflicted severe shocks on the economy of Ross and Cromarty and have exposed the vulnerability of many of its communities (HIDB, 1990).

Within Ross and Cromarty there are distinct economic and cultural characteristics associated with the east and west of the district. West Ross is a predominantly crofting economy with its cultural identity firmly rooted in the Gaelic tradition. Fishing and tourism are the two other strengths of the West Ross economy, and in recent years fish farming has grown to be of major importance. In common with most other parts of the Highlands and Islands the public sector is a significant local employer in West Ross.

2. Employment Structure

The most recent guides to employment structures in Ross and Cromarty are from the Census of Employment undertaken in September 1984 and 1987. The results are tabulated below.

Table 4.3 - Employment Structure in Ross and Cromarty, 1984 and 1987.		
	1984	1987
Percentage of employees in:		
Agriculture, Forestry and Fishing	5.6	4.5
Energy and Water Supply	1.7	2.0
(Total Primary Sector)	(7.3)	(6.5)
Manufacturing Sector	16.3	17.4
Construction Sector	15.1	7.9
Service Sector	61.3	68.2
Total Employees*	13,634	13,174
	59% male	57% male
	41% female	43% female

(Source: Census of Employment* 1984 & 1987).

*The Census of Employment is for employees only and thus excludes the self-employed which are a significant part of the work force, especially in West Ross.

As the above figures are the average for Ross and Cromarty, in addition to excluding the self-employed, they also fail to show the importance of primary sector employment to the citizens of Gairloch and West Ross. This results in there being a greater number of jobs in the East, a smaller proportion of which are in the primary sector (HIDB, 1990).

Nationally, employment trends are characterised by a rising percentage share of female employees and an increasing proportion of part-time working. In 1984, 41% of all employees in Ross and Cromarty were female, and this had risen only slightly to 43% by 1987. Although this mirrors the national trend, movement in Ross and Cromarty is only marginal. The proportions of full- and part-time female employees remained static between 1984 and 1987, with the majority of female employment being full-time (HIDB, 1990).

Details for the self-employed are available only from the 1981 Census of Population. As a percentage of the economically active population (males 16 - 65 and females 16 - 60), 24.7% of males and 11.2% of females were self-employed in West Ross. This high proportion of self-employed people reiterates the importance of traditional primary sector industries of crofting and fishing to West Ross.

3. *Economic Activity*

These figures show the percentages of males aged 16 - 65 and females aged 16 - 60 who were economically active in West Ross and the Highlands and Islands Development Board area in 1981.

Table 4.4 - Economic Activity Rates (males 16 - 65 and females 16 - 60) in West Ross and HIDB area (%), 1981.		
Percentage of Economically Active (males 16 - 65 and females 16 - 60)	West Ross	HIDB
Male	94.4	94.8
Female	53.4	57.4
(Source: Census of Population 1981).		

4. *Unemployment*

The unemployment percentages for Gairloch Parish in April each year from 1986 to 1990 (HIDB, 1990) are similar to the contemporary Highland Region figures (Department of Employment). However, the unemployment rates in Gairloch are consistently higher than the average figures quoted for West Ross (HIDB, 1990).

The figures for Gairloch Parish, West Ross and Highland Region are tabulated below.

Table 4.5 - Unemployment Percentage, Gairloch Parish, West Ross and Highland Region (%), 1986 - 1990.					
Unemployment Percentage	1986	1987	1988	1989	1990
Gairloch Parish	15.2	18.0	14.2	11.3	8.8
West Ross	12.5	15.9	12.4	9.6	7.8
Highland Region	16.1	15.7	14.7	10.5	8.2
Figures quoted are for April in any given year.					
(Source: HIDB, 1990).					

The seasonal effects on the unemployment figures in West Ross, due to the influence of tourism, are quite marked. The male, female and total unemployment rates for West Ross between 1985 and 1989 are shown graphically below.

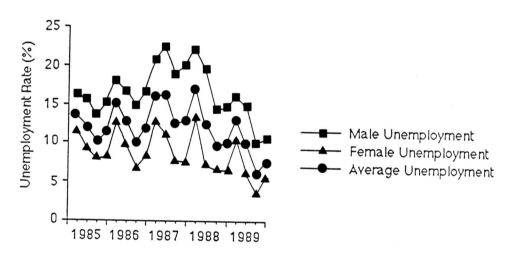

Figure 4.2 - Male, female and total unemployment rates for West Ross between 1985 and 1989 (Source: HIDB, 1990)

Although the seasonal employment trends are apparent for both men and women, fluctuations in the unemployment rate are even more conspicuous for the female work force.

5. Employment Characteristics of Gairloch Parish

Gairloch Parish, in common with West Ross, is a traditional community with a strong dependence on primary sector industries. Crofting represents an important element in the area's agricultural structure and the main activities are rearing sheep and beef cattle. There is a small port at Gairloch village which is an important shellfish port. A large proportion of the landed shellfish catch is bought by the fish processors, Gairloch Seafoods and Amazon Seafoods, who are both major employers on the west coast. The local fishing fleet based at Gairloch is small and concentrates on shellfish. There are also two fish farming enterprises in the area, each employing around five people. The local authority is also a major local employer, providing employment at the schools, Gairloch nursing home and also as manual workers.

There are limited opportunities for regular full-time or part-time work for women, and many of these jobs are located in or near Gairloch Village. The schools, bank, nursing home, shops, doctor's surgery and tourist office all employ women on a regular basis.

Tourism is a particularly significant factor in the economy of the Gairloch area. This provides much seasonal work, mostly for women, as kitchen or domestic staff at local hotels and restaurants, with additional jobs also being made available at the tourist centre, museum, Inverewe Gardens (at Poolewe) and local shops.

CHILDCARE SERVICES

There are no local authority or private sector day nursery or creche facilities in Gairloch Parish. The only registered childminder no longer provides this service, however, another woman is currently undergoing the registration process.

Pre-school children in Kinlochewe and Gairloch have no access to nursery education, but those living in or around Aultbea, Poolewe and Inverasdale have the opportunity to attend one or two nursery classes each week as part of a Highland Region 'experiment' in peripatetic nursery education provision. This project is described further in Appendix 1. Although Kinlochewe Primary School has no nursery education, it is participating in another Highland Region project known as PALS (Play and Learning Sessions). This encourages all children in their pre-school year to visit the primary school for one afternoon per week from February until the end of the summer term. At the end of each session each child is receives a pre-school pack of books and toys which they return and exchange the following week (see Appendix 1 for further details of this project).

There are four playgroups at Aultbea, Poolewe and two in Gairloch - one English and one Gaelic speaking. There are also mother & toddler groups in each of these three villages. Pre-school children from Inverasdale attend facilities in Poolewe. Kinlochewe currently has no mother & toddler group or playgroup.

The numbers of places available at the different facilities for pre-school children throughout Gairloch Parish are tabulated below (Table 4.6).

Table 4.6 - Provision of Places for Pre-school Children in Gairloch Parish.			
	Nursery Class (1 session/wk)	**Playgroup**	**Mother & Toddler**	**Total**
Aultbea	10[1]	20	10	40
Gairloch	-	40[2]	15	
		10[3]		65
Inverasdale	10[1]	-	-	10
Kinlochewe	-	-	-	-
Poolewe	10[1]	15	10	35

1 Although there are nursery places for 10 children in their pre-school year at each session, at Aultbea there are 12 such children so the nursery teacher receives additional support. At Inverasdale and Poolewe there are less children in this age-group, so these sessions are undersubscribed.

2 English speaking playgroup.

3 Gaelic speaking playgroup, currently re-registering for greater numbers of children.

In theory there are around 140 pre-school places for children at the three nursery class sessions, playgroups and mother & toddler groups in the area. However, not all groups are running at full capacity. For example, although there are (in theory) nursery places for ten children in their pre-school year at each session, there are only two children in this age-group at Inverasdale and only four Poolewe, so these six children have the opportunity to attend two nursery classes each week at both Inverasdale and Poolewe. The Gairloch English speaking playgroup is registered for 20 children, but when demand exceeded this it started running two playgroup sessions a day and caters for a total of 30 rather than a possible 40 pre-school children). Running at full capacity is not due to a lack of interest, but because there are sometimes too few children in the targeted age-group to fill all the places at a particular service.

Many of the pre-school children, especially aged between 3 and 5, often attend more than one of the services in the area. This, together with the fact that not all 150 places available at the different facilities for pre-school children are being utilised, means that not all of the estimated 130 pre-school children in Gairloch Parish are attending any form of pre-school provision.

The numbers of pre-school services in Gairloch, calculated as full-time equivalents (FTE) per 1,000 of the Gairloch population aged 0 - 4, are contrasted with those for Highland Region and Scotland below.

Table 4.7 - FTE Pre-school Places per 1,000 of the population aged 0 - 4 (and per 1,000 of population aged 3 - 4) in Gairloch Parish, Highland Region and Scotland.			
FTE places per 1,000 of population aged 0 - 4 (3 - 4)	Gairloch Parish	Highland Region[1]	Scotland[1]
Nursery Education	23 (69)	48 (119)	68 (170)
Local Authority Day Nursery	0	2	16
Childminder	23	43	37
Private Day Nursery	0	—	5
Playgroup	72 (180)	—	
Mother & Toddler	15	—	—

— Information not available
[1] Provisional data for 1989, Scottish Education Department

Table 4.7 shows that there are fewer FTE places for nursery education or with childminders than in either Highland Region or Scotland. Gairloch also has no local authority or private day nurseries.

The playgroup and mother & toddler facilities in each village are described below, while further details of the PALS (Play and Learning Sessions) at Kinlochewe school and the peripatetic nursery project at Aultbea, Poolewe and Inverasdale schools are given in Appendix 1.

Aultbea

All pre-school children aged between 3 and 5 in the Aultbea area attend the playgroup which meets in the village hall for two hours twice a week. The group, is registered for 20 children, and is attended by around 16 children. There is a playleader and parents take turns to assist with duties. This arrangement is difficult for those mothers in work to meet. The charges are £1 per child for each playgroup session in the term.

The Aultbea Mother & Toddler Group meets once a week, also at the village hall. It makes a charge of 75p for all children aged more than one year attending and is attended by many, but not all, mothers in the area with babies and toddlers. Some mothers who are in part-time, and all those in full-time employment, are unable to attend.

Gairloch

The Gairloch English speaking playgroup meets in a room attached to the Gairloch Community Centre. The playleader is assisted by two parent helpers and the charges are 75p per child for each session. The group is registered for up to 20 children each session, currently meets for two sessions twice a week and caters for a total of 30 children. The playleader estimates that between 8 and 10 of these children also attend the Gaelic playgroup which meets on alternate days.

Children travel to the playgroup from as far as Melvaig, 9 miles north and from Redpoint, 12 miles to the south. One of the pre-school children who attends the English

Gairloch, West Ross

speaking group is physically disabled. An assistant playleader is funded by a special needs grant from the Social Work Department for two of the two-hour sessions each week, specifically to care for this child. Apart from the specific funding for the child with special needs the playgroup receives no funding or other grants.

The Gaelic speaking playgroup in Gairloch is affiliated to the Gaelic Association of Playgroups. It meets three times a week on alternate days to the English speaking playgroup. The two groups share the same room in the community centre. One parent assists the playleader each session and fees of £1 per child are charged for each two-hour session. This playgroup is only registered for 10 children, but is currently re-registering for a greater number. It can be attended by up to 15 children each session. Between 8 and 10 of these children also attend the English speaking playgroup on alternate days. Like the other Gairloch playgroup, parents bring children from more than 10 miles away to attend this service, so access to a car is essential.

The Gaelic playgroup does not receive any funding from Highland Region Social Work Department, but has been successful in securing a £500 revenue grant from the Education Department.

The mother & toddler group at Gairloch uses the same room in the community centre as the two playgroups. The mothers & toddlers meet together one afternoon a week and there is a charge of 50p for each mother. Young families again travel as far as 9 miles south from Melvaig and 12 miles north from Redpoint. The group is usually attended by between 10 and 15 mothers, although not necessarily the same ones each week. The majority of pre-school children attending are babies or toddlers, but mothers who also have playgroup age children often bring them along as they don't usually have any alternative arrangements. Any new mothers in the area or incomers to the village are encouraged to attend by existing mother & toddler group members and the local health visitor.

Despite the fact that both the playgroups and the mother & toddler group all use the same room in the community centre, none of the groups share any equipment.

Inverasdale

There are no playgroup or mother & toddler facilities in Inverasdale. Pre-school children and their parents wishing to use these facilities travel to the neighbouring village of Poolewe, 4 miles away.

Kinlochewe

Until recently Kinlochewe had a combined mother & toddler and playgroup session each week, but this group has been temporarily suspended. There are only 5 pre-school children in the area, all of whom attended the playgroup, but three of these who will start at Kinlochewe Primary School next year are participating in the school visiting and pre-school pack scheme. Although the group will be diminished in numbers, two babies are expected in the near future. It is hoped the group will be revived, or possibly linked with the playgroup in Torridon, 10 miles away (and outside Gairloch Parish).

Poolewe

The Poolewe playgroup meets for two hours a week at Poolewe Village Hall. The playgroup is registered for 15 children aged between 3 and 5 and makes a charge of £1.50 per child. The play leader is assisted by a parent helper to undertake activities with the 10 children who attend from Poolewe and Inverasdale.

Poolewe also has a mother & toddler group that also meets in the village hall once a week. The group is usually attended by around 10 mothers and 15 children from Poolewe and Inverasdale.

1. Satisfaction with Local Childcare and Demand for New Services

Many mothers of pre-school children in Gairloch Parish expressed satisfaction with the actual services that they and their pre-school children were using. However, the majority were dissatisfied with limited hours of facilities and the limited ranges of childcare options that were available to them. Many of those women living outwith Aultbea, Gairloch and Poolewe villages said they found the facilities difficult to get to and would like closer services and/or transport to be provided for them. The majority of the women in the area were keen to see an increased range of childcare facilities available enabling them to choose the most appropriate service rather than the only one that is available.

Parents of children participating in the peripatetic nursery project in the north of the area and the Play and Learning Sessions at Kinlochewe school are enthusiastic about the projects and are keen for them to continue. In contrast, parents of pre-school year children in Gairloch village were disappointed that their children had no access to nursery education and 64% consider that this should be a priority for the future. Several mothers suggested that a nursery class should be incorporated into the designs of the new primary and secondary schools currently being planned for Gairloch.

In addition to nursery education being more widely available, 64% of women surveyed would like a local authority day nursery to be set up in the area, and 16% would like to see an increased number of registered childminders. Of the women currently in paid employment, most preferred the idea of a local authority day nursery, but 16% suggested that a workplace nursery would be better for their needs. 18% of all the women in the area would like to see the development of holiday play schemes and 10% would like local pre- and after-school clubs.

THE RURAL CHILDCARE SURVEY - METHODOLOGY

A questionnaire survey was undertaken in the four areas involved in this research. The objectives of the survey were to collate social and economic characteristics of the households, together with details of pre-school children, pre-school services used, satisfaction with these services and preferred service.

600 questionnaires were distributed between the four survey areas. The questionnaires were circulated through mother & toddler groups, playgroups, nursery education classes in Buckie & Rathford Lennox EDs, Brae & Ollaberry, and Gairloch, and through mother & toddler groups, playgroups and a private day nursery in Donside. It is recognised that a fault with this method of sampling is that all the families reached by the questionnaire would have been using some form of childcare service each week, but time constraints did not enable other methods of circulation.

The questionnaire was quite lengthy and comprised four sections. Mothers of pre-school children were asked to complete the first section (giving general information and details of their use of and satisfaction with childcare services) and then one of the three subsidiary sections depending on whether they were currently in paid work, undertaking some form of education or training course or doing neither of these. Lone fathers with pre-school children were asked only to complete the first section.

Of the 600 questionnaires, only 504 were actually distributed to parents of pre-school children, and a total of 267 (275 including late returns) were completed. The numbers distributed and completed in each area are as follows:

	No. of questionnaires circulated	No. of questionnaires returned	Response rate (%)
Buckie & Rathford Lennox EDs, Grampian Region	211	104	49%
Donside ED, Grampian Region	158	97	61%
Gairloch Parish, Highland Region	78	39	50%
Brae & Ollaberry, Shetland	57	27	47%
Total	504	267	53%

There were also 8 questionnaires which were returned too late to be included in the analysis, making a final total of 54% of questionnaires returned.

The data from the 267 questionnaires were analysed by computer, and some of the key findings are presented in this chapter.

In all the tables the figures represent column percentages unless otherwise stated.

☆ represents less than 1%.

Chapter 5

FINDINGS OF THE RURAL CHILDCARE SURVEY

PROFILE OF HOUSEHOLDS

1. *Number of children (aged 0 - 16) per household*

Although the numbers of children aged 0 - 16 in the households surveyed ranged from one to five, the most common number of children per household in all four of the survey areas was two. The average number of children per household across all the four survey areas was also two.

2. *Number of pre-school children*

The most common number of pre-school children in each family in all four survey areas was one (average 58%) with 40% of the families having two pre-school children (Table 5.1b). Three families in Donside ED had three pre-school children, along with two families in Gairloch and one in Shetland. The average number of pre-school children was similar in the four survey area at 1.4 children per family.

3. *Age structure of pre-school children*

The survey identified more pre-school children in the three to five age range than in the zero to two age range in every survey area except Shetland (Table 5.1c). This is more likely to reflect the attendance at pre-school services and method of the questionnaire distribution than a falling birth rate. This suggests that three to five year olds were more likely to be participating in some pre-school service than those aged two or younger.

4. *Expectant mothers*

The survey identified a total of 34 mothers who are expecting another child (Table 5.1d). These represented 10% of women responding to the questionnaire in Buckie & Rathford Lennox EDs, and 14% to 15% in the other three survey areas.

5. *Adults in the household*

All the questionnaires from the four areas were completed by women. Hence the survey did not reach any lone fathers with pre-school children. Of the women, an average of 93% had a husband or partner, ranging from 88% in Gairloch to 96% in Shetland.

A total of 21 single mothers were identified, an average of 7% of families. Of these 2% lived with other relatives, but 5% lived in lone parent households (Table 5.1e). The Gairloch area appears to have a higher proportion of single mothers (12%), the majority of whom were living with relatives, suggesting a shortage of affordable rented accommodation in the area.

6. *Chronic health problems or disability in household*

An average of 94% of families reported no health problems or disabilities in their household (Table 5.1f). This figure was slightly lower in Buckie & Rathford Lennox EDs (92%) and higher in Gairloch and Shetland (96%).

1% of women reported they had dependent husbands and a further 1% of women reported that they themselves had long term health problems or a disability. 3% of families have a pre-school child with chronic health problems or a disability which makes looking after them difficult. The final 1% of families reported that they were responsible for caring for another relative (eg a school-age child or a grandparent) within their household.

7. *Local and incoming families*

Women were asked whether they or their husband/partner were either born or brought up in the area in which they live. This question produced widely differing responses from the four survey areas (Table 5.1g). In Buckie and Rathford Lennox EDs, 79% of families have local connections, compared to 70% in the communities of Brae & Ollaberry in Shetland. The proportions of local families are significantly lower in Gairloch and in Donside ED, where this survey identified 49% and 74% of incoming families. Such families tend to have larger incomes, and often provide the motivation to improve local services or campaign for new ones. They do, however, lack the support of extended families.

PROFILE OF HOUSEHOLDS:
TABLES 5.1 (a-g)

	Buckie & Rathford Lennox	Donside	Gairloch Parish	Brae & Ollaberry	Average
TABLE 5.1 a					
Number of children (aged 0 - 16) in each family					
1 child	25%	23%	20%	26%	24%
2 children	56%	47%	59%	48%	52%
3 children	14%	29%	13%	22%	20%
4 children	4%	1%	8%	4%	3%
5 children	1%	0%	0%	0%	☆%
Total no. of children (0 - 16)	208	202	80	56	
TABLE 5.1 b					
Number of pre-school children (0 - 5) in each family					
1 pre-school child	62%	57%	51%	55%	58%
2 pre-school children	38%	41%	44%	41%	40%
3 pre-school children	0%	2%	5%	4%	2%
Total number	143	141	60	40	
TABLE 5.1 c					
Age structure of pre-school children					
0 - 12 months	7%	10%	20%	10%	10%
13 - 24 months	15%	9%	7%	17%	12%
2 years	17%	22%	12%	25%	19%
3 years	20%	22%	28%	20%	22%
4 years	38%	36%	23%	25%	34%
5 years (but not at school)	3%	1%	10%	3%	3%
TABLE 5.1 d					
Expectant mothers in each area					
Expectant mothers	10%	14%	15%	15%	13%
TABLE 5.1 e					
Present in household in addition to mother & children					
Husband/Partner	91%	91%	88%	96%	91%
Husband & other relatives	3%	3%	0%	0%	2%
Relatives only	0%	3%	10%	4%	2%
No-one (i.e. lone mother)	6%	3%	2%	0%	5%
Total single mothers	6%	6%	12%	4%	7%

E

	Buckie & Rathford Lennox	Donside	Gairloch Parish	Brae & Ollaberry	Average

TABLE 5.1 f

Chronic health problems or disability in household					
No ill health or disability	92%	94%	96%	96%	94%
Dependent husband	1%	1%	0%	4%	1%
Mother - ill health or disability	2%	2%	0%	0%	1%
Pre-5 child with ill health or disability	4%	2%	3%	0%	3%
Other dependent relative (eg older child or grandparent)	1%	1%	3%	0%	1%

TABLE 5.1 g

One or both parents local to area					
Local	79%	36%	51%	70%	58%
Non-local	21%	64%	49%	30%	42%

SOCIO-ECONOMIC CHARACTERISTICS OF HOUSEHOLDS

1. Income

An average 8% of all the families surveyed were living on a weekly household income of less than £80, with a further 11% having an income of between £81 and £120 (Table 5.2 a). These 19% of families all have household incomes below half the average for Scotland (£234 per week in 1988, Regional Trends No. 25, 1990) and are clearly living at unacceptably low levels of income. The proportions were slightly lower in Buckie & Rathford Lennox EDs (17%) and Donside ED (16%), but were significantly higher in Gairloch (20%). A further 15% of families have a household income of less than £160 per week.

A total of 45% of families have household incomes below £200 per week, but there are marked differences between the four areas surveyed. In Gairloch 66% of families had income of less than £200, compared with Shetland (48%), Buckie & Rathford Lennox EDs (45%) and Donside ED (36%). All of these data indicate that a significant proportion of families with pre-school children in rural areas are currently living in or likely to experience poverty.

Despite 19% of families having incomes of less than £120, 90% of the families surveyed owned a car. This suggests that car ownership is correlated more strongly with remoteness than household prosperity. In turn the outlay on purchase, maintenance and running costs may well prejudice other aspects of quality of life.

2. Age of mother

There are marked differences in the age structures of the mothers from the four survey areas. On average 15% were aged below 26, but the proportions ranged from 6% in Donside ED to 48% in the communities of Brae and Ollaberry in Shetland (Table 5.2 b).

The age structures of mothers in Donside ED and Gairloch were significantly older than in the other survey areas, with 62% and 57% aged over 31, compared with 44% in Buckie & Rathford Lennox EDs and only 26% in Shetland.

3. Education of the mother

Only 8% of mothers in Donside ED have no school qualifications compared to 20 - 22% of women in the other three survey areas. An average of 43% of the mothers highest school qualification was one or more O-grades. An average of 40% had Highers or A-levels, but this varied from 22% in Shetland and 34% in Buckie & Rathford Lennox EDs, up to 49 - 50% in Gairloch and Donside ED (Table 5.2 c).

54 - 55% of women in Buckie & Rathford Lennox EDs, Gairloch or Shetland had no post-school qualifications, contrasting with only 35% of those in Donside ED. The proportions of women in Gairloch and Donside ED gaining a college diploma, HND or degree were 34% and 37%, compared with 17% of those in Buckie & Rathford Lennox EDs and only 14% in Shetland (Table 5.2 d). The greater numbers of post-school qualifications in Gairloch and Donside ED are also correlated with the greater proportions of incomers to those areas. This suggests that all four survey areas lack opportunities for women to undertake post-school training or education. As a result training needs of these women, particularly in isolated areas such as Shetland and Gairloch, are likely to be higher.

4. *Working status prior to birth of first child*

Prior to the birth of their first child an average of 91% of the women surveyed were in paid employment, 2% were participating in an education course or training scheme and 7% were doing neither of these (Table 5.2 e). Although the average figures were consistent for the areas surveyed in Grampian and Highland Region, in Brae & Ollaberry (Shetland), there were fewer women in paid employment (65%) and greater proportions in education or training (11%) with 23% involved in neither. It is possible that women involved in crofting did not consider themselves to be in paid employment.

5. *Working pattern prior to birth of first child*

Of the women in paid employment, prior to the birth of their first child, 90% were working full-time compared to only 10% working part-time. Only 3% worked either in the evenings or overnight, and only 6% of women reported that they had been in temporary, casual or seasonal employment. None of the women reported having been homeworkers.

6. *Women's occupational group prior to birth of first child*

The occupational groups of the women in employment prior to the birth of their first child are listed in Table 5.2 g. 11% were in professional occupations (doctor, veterinary surgeon, optician, etc.) or teaching, with a further 26% involved in other intermediate occupations, such as nursing, social or community work, managerial work, shop keepers, hotel owner, etc.. 40% of women were routine non-manual workers (eg clerical occupations, shop or sales work) or skilled workers (hairdressers, crafts, technicians, etc.). The remaining 23% were semi- or non-skilled manual workers, such as fish factory workers, kitchen staff, waitresses, care workers, childminders, playleaders, home helps, domestic staff or farm labourers.

There were some differences between the four survey areas (Table 5.2 g) with a higher proportion in Donside ED having been in professional or intermediate occupations, and a greater proportion of those in Gairloch in semi- or non-skilled manual work.

7. Current working status of mother

Although this is discussed in more detail later in the report, it can be noted that an average of 36% of the women were in paid employment, ranging from 29% in Buckie & Rathford Lennox EDs to 38% in Donside ED, 41% in Gairloch and 44% in Shetland. Only 1% of the women (Table 5.2 h) regarded themselves as participating in any education or training at the time of the survey. The remaining 63% of women were in neither paid work nor participating in any education or training. Of those mothers in employment 16% were working full-time and 84% part-time. 15% worked evenings or overnight, and 18% were in casual, temporary or seasonal work.

8. Informal childcare arrangements for pre-school children

Women were asked whether, in addition to using childcare services, they were able to make any informal childcare arrangements for their pre-school children. 33% of the women indicated they did not or were not able to make any such informal arrangements (Table 5.2 i). An average of 45% said that their husbands/partners were willing to help. 46 - 48% of women in Buckie & Rathford Lennox EDs, Gairloch and Shetland received assistance from relatives, but this fell to 33% of women in Donside ED, reflecting the large proportion of incomers in this area. An average of 22% of women made informal childcare arrangements with friends or neighbours. In Donside ED this figure was substantially higher at 29%.

SOCIO-ECONOMIC CHARACTERISTICS OF HOUSEHOLDS:

TABLES 5.2 (a-i)

	Buckie & Rathford Lennox	Donside	Gairloch Parish	Brae & Ollaberry	Average

TABLE 5.2 a

Average household income per week (including benefits)					
Less than £80	8%	7%	11%	12%	8%
£ 81 - £120	9%	9%	18%	8%	11%
£121 - £160	16%	13%	24%	8%	15%
£161 - £200	12%	7%	13%	20%	11%
£201 - £250	21%	16%	11%	24%	18%
£251 - £300	12%	9%	8%	4%	10%
£301 - £350	9%	12%	2%	12%	9%
More than £351	13%	27%	13%	12%	18%

TABLE 5.2 b

Age of Mother					
Less than 20	0%	0%	2%	0%	☆%
21 - 25	16%	6%	13%	48%	15%
26 - 30	40%	32%	28%	26%	34%
31 - 35	35%	43%	39%	15%	37%
35+	9%	19%	18%	11%	14%

TABLE 5.2 c

Education - highest school qualification					
No qualifications	22%	8%	20%	22%	17%
O-grades	44%	42%	31%	56%	43%
Highers/A-levels	34%	50%	49%	22%	40%

TABLE 5.2 d

Education - highest post-school qualification					
No qualifications	54%	35%	54%	55%	47%
Scotvec/City & Guilds	15%	8%	2%	26%	12%
Secretarial	7%	11%	5%	4%	7%
Nursing Certificate	7%	9%	5%	4%	8%
HND/College Diploma	8%	11%	21%	7%	11%
Degree/Higher Degree	9%	26%	13%	4%	15%

	Buckie & Rathford Lennox	Donside	Gairloch Parish	Brae & Ollaberry	Average
TABLE 5.2 e					
Working status prior to birth of first child					
In paid work	96%	91%	95%	65%	91%
In education or training	0%	2%	0%	11%	2%
Not working or training	4%	7%	5%	23%	7%
TABLE 5.2 f					
Working pattern prior to birth of first child					
Full-time	90%	87%	92%	100%	90%
Part-time	10%	13%	8%	0%	10%
Evenings/Overnight	3%	5%	3%	0%	3%
Temporary/Casual/Seasonal	2%	6%	19%	0%	6%
TABLE 5.2 g					
Women's occupational group prior to birth of first child					
1) Professional occupations	3%	5%	0%	0%	3%
2) Teachers	6%	10%	11%	6%	8%
3) Nursing, medical, social	11%	16%	6%	11%	12%
4) Intermediate non-manual	7%	18%	20%	11%	14%
5) Clerical occupations	20%	26%	11%	50%	23%
6) Shop assistant and sales	17%	7%	3%	5%	10%
7) Skilled occupations	10%	7%	3%	0%	7%
8 - 11) Semi- and non-skilled	26%	11%	46%	17%	23%
TABLE 5.2 h					
Current working status of mother					
In paid work	29%	38%	41%	44%	36%
In education or training	1%	0%	2%	0%	1%
Not working or training	70%	62%	57%	56%	64%
TABLE 5.2 i					
Informal childcare arrangements for pre-school children					
None	34%	33%	32%	33%	33%
Husbands/Partner	44%	47%	37%	59%	45%
Relatives	46%	33%	47%	48%	41%
Friends/Neighbours	17%	29%	24%	18%	22%

PUBLIC AND PRIVATE TRANSPORT

1. Public transport

In all cases the nearest form of public transport was either a bus or a post bus. 70% of all women surveyed reported that it took less than 10 minutes to walk to the nearest bus service (Table 5.3 a). This fell to 49% of those in Donside ED, where 38% of women said they would have to walk for more than 20 minutes (substantially more in many cases) to reach the nearest bus service.

Buckie & Rathford Lennox EDs have by far the most frequent bus services with 85% of women indicating there was a service at least once an hour. This compares with 12% in Donside ED and none in Gairloch and Shetland (Table 5.3 b). In contrast 62% in Donside ED, 88% in Shetland and all of the women in Gairloch reported the bus service was less frequent than every two hours. The only bus service available in Gairloch runs once a day in each direction.

Few of the women surveyed made frequent use of their local bus service, 85% saying they never or very rarely used the service. Even in Buckie & Rathford Lennox EDs where most of women have access to an hourly bus service, only 19% used the service one or more times per week (Table 5.3 c).

2. Car ownership and access

All four survey areas had high proportions of car ownership households. The average was 90%, but this varied from 83% in Buckie & Rathford Lennox EDs to 99% of the families in Donside ED. 90% of mothers surveyed indicated that they were able to drive. This ranged from 82% of those in Gairloch up to 98% of those in Donside (Tables 5.3 d and e).

71% of mothers reported that they regularly had access to a car during the daytimes. There are significant differences across the four survey areas, with 56% of mothers in Ollaberry & Brae, Shetland reporting regular access in contrast to 82% in Donside ED. There is more continuity between the survey areas when comparing either occasional or regular daytime access to a car. The average figure rises to 88%, suggesting that most women can have access during the daytime if they need one. Only 6% of mothers surveyed said that they never had any access to the use of a car during the daytimes or evenings. This was lowest in Donside at 1% and highest in Buckie & Rathford Lennox EDs at 12% (Table 5.3 f).

PUBLIC AND PRIVATE TRANSPORT: TABLES 5.3 (a-f)

	Buckie & Rathford Lennox	Donside	Gairloch Parish	Brae & Ollaberry	Average
TABLE 5.3 a					
How long to walk to nearest public transport					
Less than 10 minutes	89%	49%	64%	82%	70%
10 - 20 minutes	7%	13%	26%	11%	12%
More than 20 minutes	4%	38%	10%	7%	18%
TABLE 5.3 b					
Frequency of nearest public transport					
15 minute service	3%	0%	0%	0%	1%
30 minute service	11%	1%	0%	0%	5%
Hourly service	71%	11%	0%	0%	33%
Two hourly service	10%	26%	0%	12%	14%
Less frequent than 2 hours	5%	62%	100%	88%	47%
TABLE 5.3 c					
Use of public transport					
Daily	1%	0%	0%	0%	☆%
3 - 4 times a week	5%	0%	2%	4%	3%
1 - 2 times a week	13%	12%	8%	11%	12%
Never/Rarely	81%	88%	90%	85%	85%
TABLE 5.3 d					
Car ownership households					
Car	83%	99%	85%	93%	90%
No car	17%	1%	15%	7%	10%
TABLE 5.3 e					
Mother able to drive					
Mother can drive	86%	98%	82%	89%	90%
Mother not able to drive	14%	2%	18%	11%	10%
TABLE 5.3 f					
Mother's access to a car					
Regularly daytimes	67%	82%	62%	56%	71%
Occasionally daytimes	16%	9%	26%	33%	17%
Total - some daytime access	83%	91%	88%	89%	88%
No access - days or evenings	12%	1%	8%	4%	6%

WORKING MOTHERS

1. Current working status of mother

An average of 36% of the mothers surveyed were in paid employment, 29% in Buckie & Rathford Lennox EDs, rising to 38% in Donside ED, 41% in Gairloch and 44% in Shetland (Table 5.4a). These figures are high - in three of the four areas studied - when compared to the 1988 GB average of 36% of women with children aged under five in full-time or part-time work (OPCS, 1990). While economic activity rates for women with dependent children are rising nationally, it would appear they are higher in rural than in urban areas.

The proportion of all mothers with pre-school children aged 3 - 5 in work was greater at 45% (Table 5.4 b) than for mothers with children aged less than three (28%). A similar pattern is seen among mothers with one or more pre-school children. 45% of those with one child were in paid employment compared with 23% of women with two or more pre-school children.

2. Working patterns of mothers

Of those in employment 16% were working full-time and 84% part-time. 15% worked evenings or overnight, and 18% were in casual, temporary or seasonal work. An average of 8% were homeworkers. There were no significant differences in the patterns of working between mothers with children aged from 0 - 2, those with pre-school children aged 3 - 5, or those working mothers with one or more pre-school children (Table 5.4 c).

3. Occupational groups of working mothers

There are higher proportions of working mothers with professional occupations and in teaching, than there were amongst all the women prior to having children. 80% of these women returned to the same type of work, although not necessarily at the same level as they were previously (Tables 5.4 d and 5.4 e). Many women in these occupational groups were able to afford full-time professional childcare, but others relied on other arrangements, such as family sometimes combined with nursery education to meet the gap.

In contrast the survey recorded a decrease in the proportions of women in other intermediate or routine non-manual occupations with 27% and 26% respectively returning to work. There is a relative increase in the proportion of women undertaking semi- and non-skilled manual work, suggesting that as many as 52% of women in these occupational groups prior to having children have returned to work. However, this figure more probably reflects that some women who were previously in higher occupational groups are taking semi- and non-skilled manual work either because they are able to fit childcare around such work or there is a lack of other local job opportunities.

4. Level of work

Mothers in paid employment were asked how their current job compared with the one they had prior to having children (Table 5.4 e). An average of 18% considered their current job to be at a higher level of responsibility while a further 44% suggested their work was at a similar level. In contrast 38% considered their current job to be at a lower level than the one they had previously. When asked to select two reasons why their work was at a lower level, a majority of women (53%) suggested the lack of local, suitable and/or affordable childcare; 41% the lack of other local job opportunities; 40% said the hours and conditions of their previous job were unsuitable; and 16% stated that a lack of maternity leave arrangements had prevented their return to the same job.

> **"The cost of transport to previous employment combined with the cost of childcare meant that returning to that job was not economically viable. My current job is more local, but not at the same level as before."** Milton of Cushine, Donside ED.

5. Interval between birth of last child and returning to work

An average of 43% of women returned to work less than one year after the birth of their last child, 36% returned between one and two years later, while the remaining 21% returned three or more years afterwards. The pattern was similar in both Donside ED and Buckie & Rathford Lennox EDs, but in Gairloch women appear to return to work sooner, and in Shetland later (Table 5.4 g). When the return to work interval was compared with the women's occupational groups (Table 5.4 h) 64% of women in professional and intermediate occupations returned to work after less than 12 months, compared with 44% in routine non-manual occupations and 22% of those in semi- or unskilled work.

6. Educational qualifications of working mothers

In comparison with the educational achievements of all the women surveyed, those in work appear to have similar school qualifications, but overall they appear to have slightly more post-school qualifications (Tables 5.4 i and j). Significantly there is a decrease in those with no post-school qualifications, and an increase in those having an HND, college diploma or a degree.

7. Distances travelled to work

An average of 52% of women work at or less than 2 miles from their homes (Table 5.4 k). There are differences between the survey areas with this accounting for only 31% of the women in Donside, but 91% of those in Shetland. In contrast 28% of women work more than 11 miles from home. Differences between the survey areas are apparent with 61% of women in Donside and 19% of those in Gairloch travelling more than 11 miles to work, compared to 4% in the Buckie area and none in Shetland. Two women in Donside and one in Gairloch travel to workplaces between 32 and 37 miles away. Of the women not working from home, the majority (75%) drive themselves to work, with a further 5% getting a lift in someone else's car. 18% of women walk, with only 1% using the bus and 1% cycling. Car use is significantly higher in Donside (84%) where women have further distances to travel.

8. Childcare arrangements while working

Women working full-time use an average of 32 hours per week of childcare facilities (per family) while those in part-time work used an average of 12 hours per week. Of all the women surveyed only 11% of their pre-school children ever use a daycare facility that would enable their mother to work either on a part-time or full-time basis (ie a day nursery, registered or unregistered childminders, or nanny), compared with a total of 36% of mothers with pre-school children currently working (Table 5.4 l). The daycare gap between use of services and mothers in employment is 25%, suggesting that many women are able to make informal childcare arrangements for their pre-school children. Many confirm this when listing the childcare facilities or people who most frequently looked after their pre-school children while they were at work. Overall, 49% of husbands/partners and 35% of families (usually grandparents) assisted with childcare while 35% of women sometimes or always looked after their own children while working.

> **"Because I work, my parents have a lot of responsibility looking after my son. If there were day nurseries it would relieve a lot of pressure."** Gairloch.

"It is sometimes necessary for my husband to take our daughter to work with him because of my working hours, and there is no childcare facility locally on a Saturday." Milton of Cushine, Donside ED.

"I am extremely fortunate to have my parents living both near my place of work and my child's nursery class. They care for her in the mornings and she attends nursery school in the afternoon." Portgordon, Buckie & Rathford Lennox ED.

Only 16% of women used a childminder while another 13% of women were able to leave their children at a day nursery (Donside only), nursery class, playgroup or creche while they worked. 12% of women had friends who were sometimes able to help out while a small proportion of women in Buckie & Rathford Lennox had a nanny or used unregistered paid minders.

9. Satisfaction with childcare arrangements

An average of 76% of working women said they were satisfied with the childcare arrangements while they were working (Table 5.4 m). Women living in Donside and Gairloch where there are more incoming families and little or no nursery education were less satisfied than those in Buckie & Rathford Lennox EDs and the communities of Brae & Ollaberry in Shetland. The most common reasons for dissatisfaction were: childcare too expensive; not local enough; not available in the evenings or weekends; not enough local registered childminders; relatives and friends have their own commitments and mothers don't like always having to rely on them; unable to concentrate fully on work when caring for children at the same time; and only able to undertake work in which their children can be included.

"I don't work as many hours as I would like. It is often easier to take the children with me or not to go rather than try and make other arrangements." Gairloch

"Nearest day nursery provision is about 20 miles away - too far from home and in opposite direction from my work." Sauchen, Donside ED.

"I use a registered childminder for my two children aged 2 and 4. This is very expensive if you are a single working mother like myself." Alford, Donside ED.

"The cost of paying a childminder for one child reduces local wages to a negligible amount. Paying for both children to be cared for during holidays is out of the question." Poolewe, Gairloch Parish.

10. Ideal childcare while at work

Women were asked to select no more than two types of childcare facility or arrangement they would prefer for their pre-school children while they were working. Although 76% of women claimed to be satisfied with their childcare (see above), only 13% said their ideal arrangements were their current ones (Table 5.4 n). 31% of women would like their child to be receiving nursery education and 33% suggested a day nursery. Of these over 50% said that there should be a subsidised local authority day nursery in their area.

> **"Well run subsidised daycare centre with good facilities and trained staff at a fair cost as most women's incomes are small**." Gairloch.

> **"State financed nursery especially for working mothers and single parents like myself. Where fees are charged they should be tax deductible and viewed as a necessary outlay by social security**." Alford, Donside ED.

16% of women liked the idea of a creche and 15% would prefer a workplace nursery. Childminders were selected by only 10% of women as their ideal form of childcare, and 9% would prefer their child to be cared for in the familiar surroundings of their own home. None of the women suggested they would prefer to care for their children while they were working.

An average of 9% of women said they would prefer their ideal childcare to be in their own home and 64% said near to home (Table 5.4 o). The remaining 27% suggested they would prefer the childcare to be at or near their workplace.

11. Future plans

Asked about their future plans 50% of women replied they wished to stay in the same job, while 30% would like to find a better job. 3% of women planned to start their own business and 9% would like to undertake further education or training (Table 5.4 p). 8% of working mothers said they would prefer to be full-time mothers, suggesting that they are currently working solely to increase their family's income.

Unfortunately 66% of women foresaw cost and lack of local childcare facilities as being a major barrier to their future plans (Table 5.4 q). 60% anticipated that lack of suitable job options or training facilities would stand in their way, while 17% cited lack of or cost of transport. 26% believed that they lacked the necessary skills or qualifications, and 16% currently lacked the confidence to make these future changes.

WORKING MOTHERS:
TABLES 5.4 (a-q)

	Buckie & Rathford Lennox	Donside	Gairloch Parish	Brae & Ollaberry	Average

TABLE 5.4 a

Proportion of mothers surveyed in work					
	29%	38%	41%	44%	36%

TABLE 5.4 b

Working mothers as a proportion of all those with:					
children aged under 3	18%	33%	29%	37%	28%
pre-school children aged 3, 4 or 5	40%	44%	56%	62%	45%
1 pre-school child	40%	44%	56%	53%	45%
2 or more pre-school children	16%	31%	14%	27%	23%

TABLE 5.4 c

Working patterns of mothers					
Full-time	13%	14%	31%	0%	16%
Part-time	87%	86%	79%	100%	84%
Evenings/Overnight	3%	22%	6%	30%	15%
Temporary/Casual/Seasonal	17%	14%	25%	0%	18%
Homeworking	7%	11%	6%	0%	8%

TABLE 5.4 d

Occupational groups of working mothers					
1) Professional occupations	10%	6%	0%	0%	6%
2) Teachers	17%	20%	20%	10%	18%
3) Nursing, medical, social	14%	18%	0%	0%	11%
4) Intermediate non-manual	7%	6%	13%	0%	7%
5) Clerical occupations	14%	12%	13%	40%	16%
6) Shop assistant and sales	14%	9%	0%	0%	8%
7) Skilled occupations	0%	6%	7%	0%	3%
8 - 11) Semi- and non-skilled	24%	23%	47%	50%	31%

TABLE 5.4 e

Level of current job					
Higher level	21%	14%	20%	18%	18%
Similar level	55%	31%	53%	45%	44%
Lower level	24%	55%	27%	37%	38%

	Buckie & Rathford Lennox	Donside	Gairloch Parish	Brae & Ollaberry	Average

TABLE 5.4 f

Why current job is at a lower level					
Lack of local, suitable & affordable childcare	86%	42%	67%	67%	53%
No local job opportunities	29%	53%	0%	33%	41%
Hours & conditions of old job unsuitable	86%	26%	33%	33%	40%
No maternity leave arrangements	0%	21%	33%	0%	16%

TABLE 5.4 g

Interval between birth of last child and returning to work					
Less than one year	43%	43%	50%	36%	43%
One or two years	40%	29%	37%	46%	36%
Three or more years	17%	28%	13%	18%	21%

TABLE 5.4 h

	Professional & Intermediate	Routine non-manual	Semi- & non-skilled
How soon mother returned to work by occupational group			
Less than one year	64%	44%	22%
One or two years	24%	48%	41%
Three or more years	12%	8%	37%

TABLE 5.4 i

	Buckie & Rathford Lennox	Donside	Gairloch Parish	Brae & Ollaberry	Average
Working mothers - highest school qualification					
No qualifications	18%	14%	18%	25%	16%
O-grades	49%	44%	12%	67%	45%
Highers/A-levels	33%	42%	70%	8%	39%

TABLE 5.4 j

Working mothers - highest post-school qualification					
No qualifications	40%	33%	42%	59%	38%
Scotvec/City & Guilds	15%	11%	0%	25%	13%
Secretarial	3%	14%	0%	0%	6%
Nursing Certificate	9%	11%	6%	8%	10%
HND/College Diploma	15%	11%	23%	8%	14%
Degree/Higher Degree	18%	20%	29%	0%	19%

	Buckie & Rathford Lennox	Donside	Gairloch Parish	Brae & Ollaberry	Average
TABLE 5.4 k					
Distances travelled to work (one way)					
At home/less than ^{1}/2 mile	10%	17%	44%	9%	19%
^{1}/2 - 2 miles	48%	14%	12%	82%	33%
3 - 5 miles	24%	3%	12%	9%	12%
6 - 10 miles	14%	5%	13%	0%	8%
11 - 20 miles	4%	55%	13%	0%	25%
More than 21 miles	0%	6%	6%	0%	3%
TABLE 5.4 l					
Childcare arrangements while working					
Myself	10%	20%	38%	9%	35%
Husband/Partner	37%	57%	31%	54%	49%
Family	63%	26%	38%	54%	35%
Friends	13%	17%	6%	45%	12%
Nursery, playgroup, creche	17%	17%	6%	0%	13%
Registered childminder	13%	20%	19%	0%	16%
Nanny	3%	0%	0%	0%	1%
Unregistered paid minder	10%	0%	0%	0%	3%
TABLE 5.4 m					
Satisfaction with childcare while working					
Satisfied	93%	70%	56%	82%	76%
TABLE 5.4 n					
Ideal childcare arrangements while working					
Satisfied with current care	14%	17%	8%	0%	13%
Nursery education	14%	26%	69%	20%	31%
Day nursery	19%	22%	38%	30%	33%
Creche	19%	13%	15%	20%	16%
Workplace nursery	24%	0%	16%	50%	15%
Registered childminder	14%	4%	8%	25%	10%
Care at home (family, minder, nanny or sitter)	9%	13%	8%	0%	9%
TABLE 5.4 o					
Ideal childcare would be					
At home	9%	13%	8%	0%	9%
Near home	78%	48%	65%	70%	64%
At or near workplace	13%	39%	27%	30%	27%

F

	Buckie & Rathford Lennox	Donside	Gairloch Parish	Brae & Ollaberry	Average
TABLE 5.4 p					
Ideal future plans					
Stay in the same job	67%	44%	50%	27%	50%
Get a better job	27%	41%	13%	27%	30%
Start a business	0%	3%	6%	9%	3%
More education or training	3%	6%	13%	28%	9%
Be a full-time mother	3%	6%	18%	9%	8%
TABLE 5.4 q					
Barriers to future plans					
Lack of childcare	63%	71%	60%	60%	66%
Lack of suitable local job or training opportunities	38%	71%	60%	60%	60%
Lack of skills/qualifications	25%	18%	20%	60%	26%
Transport difficulties/costs	13%	24%	0%	20%	17%
Lack of confidence	0%	12%	20%	0%	9%

NON-WORKING MOTHERS

1% of the women with pre-school children surveyed were participating in an education course, while an average of 64% were neither in paid employment nor undertaking any education or training.

Only two women (one in Buckie & Rathford Lennox and the other in Gairloch) suggested that education was currently their main occupation. One was participating in a vocational course at school and the other was continuing to work through an Open University course (Table 5.5 a). It seems that a minority of the other women were undertaking part-time courses (usually vocational community education courses), but did not consider these their 'main occupation'.

As so few women were in training, the remainder of this section considers the information drawn together about the 64% of women who were neither in education nor paid employment. They will be referred to throughout as non-working mothers.

1. Profile of non-working mothers and their pre-school children

55% of all mothers with pre-school children aged between 3 and 5 were not working, but this rises to 73% of mothers with a child aged less than three (Table 5.5 b). Similarly 55% of mothers with only one pre-school child were not working, while 77% of mothers with two or more children of pre-school age were not in paid employment (Table 5.5 c).

2. Previous experience of employment

86% of non-working mothers were in paid employment immediately before the birth of their first child. Since that time an average of 45% have undertaken some form of paid employment. Fewer women (38%) in Buckie & Rathford Lennox EDs had returned to work, while 64% had undertaken paid employment.

3. Patterns of most recent paid employment

The length of their last paid job ranged from less than 1 month up to more than 5 years. On average most had spent more than one year in their last position, but in Gairloch 43% of women had only been employed for between 0-6 months (Table 5.5 d). This suggests that work available in Gairloch is more likely to be seasonal than permanent, which is confirmed by their working patterns.

Of those employed since becoming mothers, 33% reported that their last job had been full-time, compared to 67% who worked part-time. 17% (36% in Gairloch) had worked in the evenings or overnight, and 34% (50% in Gairloch) had been in temporary, casual or seasonal work. Only an average of 3% had been home workers (Table 5.5 e). Many of these women had stopped work either prior to the birth of another child or because employment was only available on a seasonal basis. Several women with two pre-school children suggested that childcare for one child is affordable, but is prohibitive for two.

> "**The cost of childcare (for two pre-school children) is so expensive that it outweighs the feasibility of working. It is so expensive - £1.50 minimum per child per hour - that I have to put off returning to work until the children are older**." Alford, Donside ED.

4.   Occupational groups

The occupational groups listed by non-working women as their most recent form of employment reflects some similarity to those listed by all the women prior to having children (Table 5.5 f). There were, however, a smaller proportion of women in professional and intermediate occupational groups and a greater portion who had undertaken semi-skilled and non-skilled manual work. This trend is particularly marked in both Gairloch and in Brae & Ollaberry, Shetland. In Gairloch this is because many women are recruited for catering, kitchen and domestic work by the hotels, restaurants and holiday chalets during the holiday season.

5.   Educational qualifications of non-working mothers

In comparison with the educational achievements of all the women surveyed, those currently not working have similar school qualifications, although there is a small increase in the proportion with no post-school qualifications (from 47% to 52%) compared to only 38% of those women currently in paid employment (Tables 5.5 h - j). There are similar proportions of women with Scotvec modules, secretarial qualifications and nursing certificates, but slightly reduced proportions of those with HNDs, college diplomas or degrees. Despite this these women as a group are well qualified with an average of 13% having a degree or higher degree.

6.   Childcare arrangements while participating in activities outside of the home

Women were asked to list not more than two facilities or people who looked after their pre-school children while they were participating in activities outside their homes. Overall 70% of husbands and 49% of families assisted with this task (Table 5.5 k). 17% were sometimes able to ask friends to help, but 16% of women usually had to take their children everywhere with them. Only 11% were able to participate in any activities during the time their pre-school children were at nursery, playgroup or creche, while 4% used a registered childminder, nanny or unregistered paid minder.

7. Satisfaction with childcare arrangements

An average of 86% of non-working women expressed satisfaction with their child care arrangements while they were out of their homes (Table 5.5 l). Satisfaction was lower in Gairloch (at 56%) where there are no day nursery or creche facilities and little nursery education. Those women who were dissatisfied most commonly said they didn't like always having to rely on their family or friends for childcare and that they were only able to participate in activities that included their pre-school children. Although many women expressed satisfaction with arrangements on a temporary basis, several pointed out that the lack of affordable daycare in rural areas prevents many mothers of pre-school children from returning to work.

> **"Though childcare is possible for my two small children it is difficult to arrange and make reliable."** Muir of Fowlis, Donside ED.

8. Ideal childcare while participating in activities out of the home

Women were asked to select no more than two types of childcare facility or arrangement they would prefer for their pre-school children while they were out of the home (Table 5.5 m). Although 86% of non-working women claimed to be satisfied with their current childcare arrangements (see above), only 24% reported that their current arrangement was their ideal form of childcare. 33% of non-working women would prefer their child to be at a day nursery, 29% at creche and 27% at nursery education. 9% of women would sometimes use a childminder, while 14% suggested family care was ideal. Only 2% of mothers suggested that playgroups would give them enough time to enable them to participate in activities without their pre-school children.

> **"A creche one or two days a week would be very handy, if it was run cheaply and near to my home. Mothers could have a few hours without the children to do a course, go shopping, etc**." Brae, Shetland.

An average of 12% of non-working women suggested their ideal childcare would be in their own home and a further 63% would prefer the care to be near to home (Table 5.5 n). 25% of non-working mothers suggested they would prefer their ideal childcare to be at or near their place of activity or training.

9. Future plans

When asked about their future plans 61% of non-working women expressed the wish to find paid employment (Table 5.5 o). 17% planned to undertake further education or training and 6% wished to run a business. Only 15% of non-working mothers planned to remain as full-time mothers and homemakers.

While 9% of non-working mothers would like to implement their future plans immediately, and 16% said when their youngest child was at playgroup or nursery, the majority (67%) planned to wait until their youngest child was at primary school (Table 5.5 p). In contrast only 6% suggested they would wait until their children were at secondary school and 2% until after their children had left home.

Non-working mothers anticipated there would be many barriers which might prevent them from undertaking their future plans. 55% anticipated that the cost of and/or lack of local childcare facilities would be their major problem.

> **"Gairloch desperately needs a full-time local authority nursery. During the summer many seasonal jobs are available but I can't apply for them because I don't have somewhere to leave the children and I can't afford to pay a full-time childminder."** Gairloch.

> **"I do not think that employers make it easy for any women with children to attend a job. If it were possible to have hours of work the same as school hours I think a lot more women would be happier."** Kemnay, Donside ED.

> **"I am one of many single mums, and feel that the cost of childcare outweighs the feasibility of working. It is so expensive per child per hour here, £1.50 minimum, that people are put off returning to work because the cost of childcare is not taken into account when benefits are worked out**." Alford, Donside.

53% of women suggested the lack of suitable local employment or training opportunities would stand in their way. 26% said they lacked the confidence, and 21% considered they did not have the necessary skills or qualifications to make these future changes (Table 5.5 q). Although 14% of non-working women believed that transport costs or difficulties would be a problem, transport issues were considered less of a barrier than the lack of local affordable childcare.

10. *Ideal child care for future plans*

29% of women anticipated that pre- and after-school care schemes would best suit their future plans, while a further 17% suggested holiday care schemes. One woman suggested that as -

> **"many jobs are seasonal, a seasonal nursery would be suitable for many mums in this area."** Gairloch.

Another 16% of women suggested that they would fit their hours of work or training around school hours (Table 5.5 r). For those women planning changes prior to their children being at primary school, childminders, day nurseries, creche and nursery education appear to fill their childcare gap.

NON-WORKING MOTHERS:
TABLES 5.5 (a-r)

	Buckie & Rathford Lennox	Donside	Gairloch Parish	Brae & Ollaberry	Average
TABLE 5.5 a					
Proportion of non-working mothers surveyed					
In education or training	1%	0%	2%	0%	1%
Not working or training	70%	62%	57%	56%	64%
TABLE 5.5 b					
Non-working mothers as a proportion of all those with:					
child/ren aged under 3	82%	67%	71%	63%	73%
pre-school child/ren aged 3, 4 or 5	60%	56%	46%	38%	55%
1 pre-school child	60%	56%	44%	47%	55%
2 or more pre-school children	84%	69%	86%	73%	77%
TABLE 5.5 c					
Undertaken paid work since birth of first child					
Yes	38%	47%	64%	47%	45%
TABLE 5.5 d					
Length of last paid employment					
0 - 6 months	18%	29%	43%	25%	27%
6 - 12 months	14%	18%	29%	13%	18%
1 - 2 years	29%	29%	14%	13%	24%
3 or more years	39%	24%	14%	49%	31%
TABLE 5.5 e					
Working pattern of last paid employment					
Full-time	22%	25%	43%	50%	33%
Part-time	78%	75%	57%	50%	67%
Evenings/Overnight	15%	11%	36%	13%	17%
Temporary/Casual/Seasonal	33%	36%	50%	0%	34%
Homeworking	4%	4%	0%	0%	3%

	Buckle & Rathford	Donside Lennox	Gairloch Parish	Brae & Ollaberry	Average
TABLE 5.5 f					
Occupational groups of working mothers					
1) Professional occupations	4%	11%	0%	0%	5%
2) Teachers	7%	0%	0%	0%	3%
3) Nursing, medical, social	7%	21%	0%	0%	10%
4) Intermediate non-manual	15%	7%	0%	0%	8%
5) Clerical occupations	19%	18%	22%	50%	22%
6) Shop assistant and sales	19%	11%	7%	12%	13%
7) Skilled occupations	3%	7%	7%	0%	5%
8 - 11) Semi- and non-skilled	26%	25%	64%	38%	34%
TABLE 5.5 g					
Undertaken training or education since birth of first child					
Yes	7%	18%	18%	7%	10%
TABLE 5.5 h					
Type of education or training					
Non-vocational	40%	27%	25%	100%	33%
Vocational	20%	73%	25%	0%	48%
O-grades/Highers	20%	0%	50%	0%	14%
Degree (OU)	20%	0%	0%	0%	5%
TABLE 5.5 i					
Non-working mothers - highest school qualification					
No qualifications	24%	5%	23%	20%	17%
O-grades	42%	41%	45%	47%	43%
Highers/A-levels	34%	54%	32%	33%	40%
TABLE 5.5 j					
Non-working mothers - highest post-school qualification					
No qualifications	61%	36%	64%	52%	52%
Scotvec/City & Guilds	15%	7%	4%	27%	12%
Secretarial	8%	9%	9%	7%	8%
Nursing Certificate	6%	7%	5%	0%	6%
HND/College Diploma	6%	11%	18%	7%	9%
Degree/Higher Degree	4%	30%	0%	7%	13%

	Buckie & Rathford Lennox	Donside	Gairloch Parish	Brae & Ollaberry	Average

TABLE 5.5 k

Childcare arrangements while participating in activities out of the house					
Myself	19%	7%	28%	15%	16%
Husband/Partner	67%	72%	56%	80%	70%
Family	54%	26%	33%	76%	49%
Friends	14%	19%	28%	8%	17%
Nursery, playgroup, creche	4%	20%	0%	0%	11%
Registered childminder	0%	0%	6%	0%	1%
Nanny	0%	2%	0%	0%	1%
Unregistered paid minder	2%	0%	1%	0%	2%

TABLE 5.5 l

Satisfaction with childcare arrangements					
Satisfied	91%	89%	56%	92%	86%

TABLE 5.5 m

Ideal childcare arrangements while participating in activities out of the house					
Satisfied with current care	36%	21%	6%	20%	24%
Nursery education	18%	36%	39%	0%	27%
Day nursery	28%	6%	75%	40%	33%
Registered childminder	2%	15%	6%	0%	7%
Creche	23%	36%	25%	40%	29%
Playgroup	2%	3%	0%	0%	2%
Care at home (minder, nanny or sitter)	0%	6%	0%	20%	3%
Family	23%	6%	6%	20%	14%

TABLE 5.5 n

Ideal childcare would be:					
At home	24%	6%	0%	0%	12%
Near home	67%	47%	79%	83%	63%
At or near workplace	9%	47%	21%	17%	25%

TABLE 5.5 o

Ideal future plans					
Get a paid job	65%	48%	73%	65%	61%
More education or training	16%	22%	4%	14%	17%
Start a business	3%	12%	9%	7%	6%
Be a full-time mother	16%	18%	14%	14%	15%

	Buckie & Rathford Lennox	Donside	Gairloch Parish	Brae & Ollaberry	Average
TABLE 5.5 p					
Ideal time to implement plans					
Now	6%	13%	13%	8%	9%
Youngest at playgroup or nursery	6%	22%	25%	33%	16%
Youngest at primary school	81%	54%	62%	50%	67%
Youngest at secondary school	7%	7%	0%	9%	6%
When children have left home	0%	4%	0%	0%	2%
TABLE 5.5 q					
Barriers to future plans					
Lack of childcare	51%	61%	71%	40%	55%
Lack of suitable local job or training opportunities	47%	55%	59%	60%	53%
Lack of confidence	31%	21%	29%	20%	26%
Lack of skills/qualifications	29%	0%	53%	20%	21%
Transport difficulties/costs	12%	15%	0%	10%	14%
TABLE 5.5 r					
Ideal childcare for future plans					
Pre- & after-school care	34%	36%	11%	9%	29%
Holiday care scheme	16%	24%	6%	9%	17%
Registered childminder	18%	14%	17%	18%	17%
Hours of work/training to suit children	21%	19%	0%	9%	16%
Day nursery	9%	7%	6%	10%	14%
Creche	18%	3%	22%	18%	13%
Nursery education	2%	10%	22%	18%	10%

CHILDCARE FACILITIES

1. *Availability of Services*

In order to get some impression of the availability of childcare facilities the women surveyed were asked what services they were aware of for pre-school children in their area. None of the survey areas have a local authority day nursery or family centre, but thereafter the similarity ends. The majority of women surveyed, 85 - 95% on the mainland and 78% in Shetland, have access to a local mother & toddler group. In Buckie & Rathford Lennox EDs 73% of the women reported pre-school children in their area had access to nursery education compared to only 7% in Donside ED and 21% in Gairloch. A higher proportion of Donside women (59%) knew of a registered childminder, contrasting with 7 - 22% in the other survey areas. A high proportion of pre-school children in Donside (95%) and Gairloch (97%) had access to a playgroup compared with only 52% in Buckie & Rathford Lennox EDs and 30% of those surveyed in Shetland. Few creche facilities were reported, except in Donside, where the Alford Community Centre make a creche available for a women's group once a week. Donside is also the only one of the four survey areas to have a private daycare facility.

2. *Use of childcare facilities*

The pattern of use of pre-school services in the four survey areas are described in this section. It must be noted however, that as the majority of questionnaires were circulated through pre-school services, attendance levels appear high. A fault of this method of sampling is that families using pre-school services were contacted, while few using no services were identified.

Tables 5.6 b, d, e, f, and g detail the use of pre-school services made by 0 - 2 year olds. The average time per week spent by the children at these services are also tabulated. On average 17% of the 0 - 2 year old children identified in the survey were not attending any form of pre-school service. This ranged from only 11 - 12% in Brae & Ollaberry, Shetland and Donside, up to 20 - 24% in Buckie & Rathford Lennox and Gairloch. Tables 5.6 e and f indicate that an average of 24% of children aged under one year were not attending compared to only 9% of two year olds. The average hours of service attendance each week also increases with age, from 2½ hours for 0 - 12 months, to 4 hours for 1 year olds, and 7 hours for 2 year olds. Age also increases the likelihood of children attending more than one service with 34% of two year olds attending two or more services, compared to 6% of those aged less than one year.

The most frequently attended service in all the survey areas was mother & toddler groups, 72% and 81% in Buckie & Rathford Lennox EDs and Donside ED. In Shetland the proportion is lower (47%) because one of the two villages surveyed (Ollaberry) had no mother & toddler group, but welcomed 0 - 2 year olds at the village playgroup. In Gairloch Parish only 33% of 0 - 2 year olds were attending any of the mother & toddler groups.

Playgroup attendance amongst the 0 - 2 age group was virtually non-existent in Buckie & Rathford Lennox EDs and Donside ED, but is very significant in Shetland and Gairloch. While the Shetland figure can be accounted for as the playgroup in Ollaberry actually caters for all pre-school children from 0 - 5, in the Gairloch area it appears that a large proportion of two year olds actually attend playgroups regularly with three to five year olds.

8% of 0 - 2 year olds are cared for by childminders. While the average number of hours per week for each of these children was only 13, the actual numbers ranged from 2 - 40 hours. The private daycare facility in Alford, Donside ED was used by 7% of 0 - 2 year olds in that area, and 2% (one child) in Buckie & Rathford Lennox EDs is cared for by an unregistered paid childminder. In total only 12% of 0 - 2 year olds were in a type of daycare facility that would enable their mother to work either on a part-time or full-time basis. This contrasts with the average of 28% of mothers of under-threes who are currently in paid employment. The daycare gap between use of services and mothers in employment is 12 - 15% in Buckie & Rathford Lennox, Donside and Gairloch, and 32% in Shetland. All of these women must either rely on family, husbands or friends for childcare or look after their own children while they are working.

The range of different childcare facilities and hours of use by pre-school children aged 3-5 are recorded in Tables 5.6 c, h, i and j. Fewer than 1% of children in this age group attended no pre-school services. As expected the number of different types of services used and total hours of provision per week for each child is also greater than those for children aged from 0 - 2.

Playgroups are the most frequently attended service in both Donside and Gairloch (92 - 97%), where the access to and hours of nursery education available are extremely limited (10 - 15% of children for 3 - 4 hours per week). In contrast in Buckie & Rathford Lennox EDs and Ollaberry & Brae, Shetland (where 63% and 74% of the 3 - 5 age group are attending nursery classes for 10 or 11 hours a week) attendance at playgroup is accordingly reduced. In these areas it is usually only the pre-school children without access to nursery education who attend the playgroups.

An average of 27% of pre-school children aged 3 - 5 are attending mother & toddler groups. In Buckie & Rathford Lennox EDs, where mother & toddler groups usually cater for all children from 0 - 5 and there are few playgroups, the proportion is particularly high at 37%.

8% of 3 - 5 year olds included in the survey were cared for by registered childminders for an average of 12 hours per week. However, the actual number of hours spent with registered childminders varied from 4 to 40. 3% of 3 - 5 year olds in Donside attended the private daycare facility, and 1% of this age group in Buckie & Rathford Lennox EDs is cared for by an unregistered childminder. A further 1% of those in both Donside and Buckie & Rathford Lennox EDs were cared for by a nanny. In total only around 11% of the 3 - 5 age group were receiving daycare at a day nursery or from registered and unregistered childminders and nannies, compared to 45% of working mothers with pre-school children aged 3 - 5 (Table 5.6 c). A minority of mothers in Buckie & Rathford Lennox EDs and Brae, Shetland might be able to fit part-time work into the two hours when their child is at nursery class each day. However, it appears that most mothers in part-time or full-time paid employment rely on their husbands, family or friends to meet the childcare gap.

> **"The services in my area do not cater for working mums. My children are cared for by their granny or my friends when I am at work**." Buckie, Buckie and Rathford Lennox ED.

3.   Satisfaction with childcare facilities

Satisfaction with childcare facilities currently being used is higher in both Buckie & Rathford Lennox (73%) and Shetland (65%), where nursery education for 3 - 5 year olds is more widely available, compared to 57% of mothers satisfied in Gairloch and 42% in Donside (Table 5.6 k).

> **"I would like my daughter of four to have more than four hours at the playgroup, as she thoroughly enjoys every minute of it**." Keig, Donside ED.

Despite saying the current service they were actually using was satisfactory, the majority of mothers surveyed made it clear that they still wanted access to a better choice of services in their local area and services for more hours each week. At the moment, the majority of mothers are using a particular childcare service "because it is the only one available", not because they have chosen to use it.

> **"Parents have no choice of facilities for their children regardless of their, and their children's needs**." Keig, Donside.

> **"There is no nursery school locally. My 4 year-old has to travel 13 miles to a nursery class of a different school than he'll attend for primary education**." Strathdon, Donside.

One quarter of the mothers surveyed in Donside said the playgroups they were using were not educational enough. This does not necessarily reflect any deficiency in these playgroups as most are actually offering a higher quality service than elsewhere. However, it does suggest that mothers in Donside are trying to fill in the gap left by no local nursery education with more educational playgroups.

> **"Playgroups are not professionally run, are operated on a very limited basis and are severely underfunded."** Donside ED.

> **"There has been no trained playleader at playgroup for last 6 months. Same activities each week and little educational value."** Donside ED.

> **"I am not criticising the playgroup. They do a good job within the boundaries of cost and staff but each child should have access to a state funded nursery class where staff are paid a good wage and are therefore generally more stable, staying for a longer period, more enthusiastic and better qualified to note any problems."** Donside ED.

> **"The playgroup is run by mothers with no playgroup leader and as a result is very disorganised."** Donside ED.

There were few comments about mother and toddler groups, but one mother reported her local group:–

> **"has little enthusiasm, is self run and funded, and contains too many smokers".** Donside.

4. Payment for childcare facilities

The total payments for childcare facilities ranged from no cost per week to 2% of families to over £41 for 5% of all families surveyed (Table 5.6 l). The largest individual payment of £65 per week is made by a working single mother in Donside with 2 children being cared for part-time by a registered childminder. There were differences in childcare costs between the four survey areas with 85% of families in Buckie & Rathford Lennox EDs and 96% in Shetland paying no more than £2 per week. In both these areas there is a high availability of nursery education (10 - 11 hours per week) for some 3 year olds and most children of 4 - 5 at minimal cost to their parents (usually £1 per week to cover the cost of a daily snack and drink). In Shetland, apart from childminders, there are only a limited amount of facilities on which to spend money as the Brae mother & toddlers group meets twice a week, while the Ollaberry playgroup only meets once.

In Donside and Gairloch (where there is limited access to nursery education for 3 or 4 hours per week), weekly childcare costs are greater. 42% of families in Donside and 36% in Gairloch pay between £3 and £10 per week, compared to 8% in Buckie & Rathford Lennox and 4% in Shetland.

8% of all families surveyed spend more than £21 each week on childcare. No families in Shetland and only 4% in Buckie & Rathford Lennox were paying more than £21, compared with 12 - 13% in Donside and Gairloch. All these families had working mothers who were paying a childminder, day nursery or nanny to care for their child/ren usually part-time, but sometimes on a full-time basis.

> **"Presently all the money I earn is spent on child care, travel to work and necessary professional fees. I work because I enjoy it and hope to do more in the future but at present there is no net income from working. I feel my childminder deserves to be paid as much as I can afford at the moment**." Keig, Donside.

There is a general correlation between weekly childcare costs, hours of childcare facilities used and family income. As expected families with larger incomes tend to have higher costs and use more hours of childcare facilities each week.

5. Ideal childcare service

All the women surveyed were asked to describe what childcare services they would ideally like to complement their existing use of facilities and other informal arrangements (Table 5.6 m). Only 16% of mothers indicated that they were "perfectly satisfied" with their current arrangements compared with the average of 59% in Table 5.6 k who were satisfied with the actual services used but would prefer more local choice.

Nursery education was identified as a priority for women in both Donside (52%) and Gairloch (70%). This was also identified by mothers of children who did not have access to local nursery education in Buckie & Rathford Lennox and Shetland.

> **"I would like to see a nursery school for my 4 year-old as she will be 5½ before she starts school and I don't feel that playgroup will keep her interest for another year**." Alford, Donside ED.

"There is no nursery school provision until age 4, and then only one morning per week until age 5. I would appreciate more nursery provision at the school, as it is an excellent introduction to school life, and makes the transition to full-time school much easier. By age 4, most children are more than ready for it." Poolewe, Gairloch Parish.

"A nursery school should be provided in the area in which I live. There are 3 primary schools within a 4 mile radius. None have nursery provision. The nearest one is in Brae which is 15 miles away." Ollaberry, Shetland.

22% of women indicated that a day nursery would best suit their needs, and of these more than 50% specifically stated that they would prefer to use a local authority day nursery to a private daycare facility.

"I would like a well run subsidised daycare centre with good facilities and trained staff at a fair cost." Gairloch.

A further 8% of women suggested that a workplace nursery would be most appropriate, while 5% would prefer to be able to use a local registered childminder. In total 35% of the women surveyed (31 - 34% in Donside and Buckie & Rathford Lennox, and 43 - 47% in Gairloch and Brae & Ollaberry) suggested a form of childcare with enough continuity that would enable them to return to the work force.

Creche facilities would be useful to 15% of the women surveyed, rising to 21% of those in Buckie & Rathford Lennox EDs and in Brae & Ollaberry, Shetland. Several of the non-working women in Shetland suggested that a creche available for one or two whole days per week would be extremely useful and enable them to undertake a part-time training course or a shopping trip to Lerwick without the pre-school children.

15% of mothers in Buckie & Rathford Lennox and 5% in Gairloch Parish suggested their pre-school child would benefit from attending a local playgroup. In Buckie this would fill a gap between mother & toddler groups and nursery education. There are playgroups in the Gairloch area but many parents and children have to travel up to 8 - 12 miles to attend, thus excluding children whose mother or parents do not have regular daytime access to a car.

6. New childcare services required

Finally, women were asked to select the two new services from a possible list of eight (Table 5.6 n). Nursery education was given the highest priority by all women whose pre-school children had no current access. An average of 39% of women would like a day nursery in their area, but this figure rose to 60% of those living in Gairloch. A typical comment was:

> "**There is a great need for both nursery education and a day nursery in this area. The nearest nursery class is 17 miles away and the nearest private nursery 22 miles away. Many children in this area live in remote locations with limited social contact. It is therefore crucial that good pre-school facilities be provided**." Keig, Donside.

Pre- and after-school care (15%) and holiday care schemes for school age children (19%) were a popular choice in all four of the survey areas. This would be of immediate benefit to working mothers who already have school age children and would enable other non-working mothers to undertake their future plans and return to the work force when their children are of primary school age.

7. *Transport to childcare facilities*

An average of 73% of the women in all the survey areas always travelled by car - either their own and/or a friend's car - when delivering their pre-school children to and collecting them from childcare facilities (Table 5.6 o). The proportion travelling by car is lower in Buckie & Rathford Lennox EDs (58%), and significantly higher in other survey areas (75 - 88%). Only 1% of women and their pre-school children ever used a bus service to travel to and from pre-school facilities.

The majority of women (85%) expressed satisfaction with their mode of transport to childcare. Those who were dissatisfied reported that as public transport is practically non-existent, it is essential to have your own transport. It is difficult for parents to attend on a regular basis if they don't have access to a car as the distance and time taken travelling to childcare services are too great.

> "**No sooner do I get home than it is time to go back and pick him up**." Gairloch Parish.

> "**At the present moment I have to travel 12 miles (24 return trip) to get to a playgroup. But there is to be a new playgroup starting in March '91 which is only 10 miles (return) and I will then go to them both once a week**." Donside.

> "**Playgroup facility only available for ages 3 and 4 on two days a week (morning sessions) and to attend other areas' playgroups involves a round trip of 20 miles**." Milton of Cushine, Donside ED.

Only a minority of women mentioned the cost of transport:-

> **"I travel 7 miles with my 5 year old to playgroup as there is nothing in my area. He could do with 3 days a week but I can't afford the petrol or the time."** Craigievar, Gordon.

> **"Because there are very limited services in the village (only a mother & toddler group), the children have to go 4 miles to Fochabers for playgroup and 6 miles to Buckie to be able to attend a nursery class and school. As there is no public transport it makes it very difficult and expensive for them to attend."** Clochan, Buckie & Rathford Lennox EDs.

More than one woman expressed concerns about shared rotas for transporting children to facilities:-

> **"It is difficult to transport my two children plus others (can be up to five) all safely restrained in the car. I often have to do a 'shuttle' trip to take all the children to and from playgroup."** Sauchen, Donside ED.

8. *Travel cost to childcare facilities*

22% of mothers surveyed did not incur any transport costs getting to or from childcare facilities. 27% estimated they spent between £1 - £2 and a further 23% between £3 - £5 (Table 5.6 q). 4% of families spent £10 - £20 per week on transport costs and 2% spent more than £21. 24% of women who travel by car did not cost this expense.

A comparison of transport costs to weekly childcare costs, indicates that the parents in rural areas appear to spend just as much, if not more, on transporting their pre-school childcare to services each week as they spent on the actual childcare facilities.

9. *Combined weekly childcare and travel costs*

Combination of the average weekly childcare and transport costs (where available) in each area, shows that the average spending per family across the four survey areas is £7.50 per week (Table 5.6 r). Those in Donside ED were spending the most, averaging £12.00 per family each week. Spending in Gairloch is also above average at £8.00 per week. In comparison families in Buckie & Rathford Lennox EDs and Ollaberry & Brae in Shetland spent between £4 - £5 on average. The differentials in spending between the survey areas result from both greater travel costs and more expensive childcare in Donside and Gairloch.

CHILDCARE FACILITIES;
TABLES 5.6 (a-r)

	Buckie & Rathford Lennox	Donside	Gairloch Parish	Brae & Ollaberry	Average

TABLE 5.6 a

Facilities in local area					
Nursery education	73%	7%	21%	59%	40%
Local authority day nursery	0%	0%	0%	0%	0%
Private day nursery	0%	31%	0%	0%	11%
Family centre	0%	0%	0%	0%	0%
Registered childminder	7%	59%	13%	22%	38%
Creche	7%	26%*	3%	0%	12%
Playgroup	52%	95%	97%	30%	72%
Mother & toddler group	88%	95%	85%	78%	89%

* Creche is only available at particular courses held Alford Community Centre

TABLE 5.6 b

Attendance and average hours per week use of pre-school childcare services by 0 - 2 year olds					
No service/attendance	20%	12%	24%	11%	17%
Private day nursery	0%	7%	0%	0%	3%
	0	30 hrs.	0	0	30 hrs.
Registered childminder	4%	11%	14%	5%	8%
	17 hrs.	11 hrs.	17 hrs.	4 hrs.	13 hrs.
Creche	4%	16%	0%	0%	7%
	2 hrs.	2 hrs.	0	0	2 hrs.
Playgroup	4%	2%	28%	42%	11%
	2 hrs.	2 hrs.	4 hrs.	2 hrs.	2 hrs.
Mother & toddler group	72%	81%	33%	47%	67%
	2 hrs.	3 hrs.	2 hrs.	4 hrs.	3 hrs.
Unregistered paid minder	2%	0%	0%	0%	1%
	49 hrs.	0	0	0	49 hrs.
Other	11%	5%	14%	0%	8%
	3 hrs.	2 hrs.	1 hrs.	0	2 hrs.
Av. no. of service hours/child	4 hrs.	5 hrs.	4 hrs.	3 hrs.	4 hrs.

	Buckie & Rathford Lennox	Donside	Gairloch Parish	Brae & Ollaberry	Average
TABLE 5.6 c					
Attendance and average hours per week use of pre-school childcare services by 3 - 5 year olds					
No service/attendance	1%	0%	0%	0%	☆
Nursery education	63%	10%	15%	74%	37%
	10 hrs.	4 hrs.	3 hrs.	10 hrs.	9 hrs
Private day nursery	0%	3%	0%	0%	1%
	0	20 hrs.	0	0	20 hrs.
Registered childminder	7%	10%	6%	10%	8%
	9 hrs.	13 hrs.	23 hrs.	6 hrs.	12 hrs.
Creche	2%	20%	0%	0%	8%
	1 hrs.	2 hrs.	0	0	2 hrs.
Playgroup	23%	92%	97%	26%	61%
	5 hrs.	5 hrs.	5 hrs.	2 hrs.	5 hrs
Mother & toddler group	37%	21%	26%	11%	27%
	2 hrs.	2 hrs.	2 hrs.	2 hrs.	2 hrs.
Nanny	1%	1%	0%	0%	1%
	40 hrs.	24 hrs.	0	0	32 hrs.
Unregistered paid minder	1%	0%	0%	0%	☆%
	49 hrs.	0	0	0	49 hrs.
Other	11%	17%	10%	5%	14%
	5 hrs.	3 hrs.	1 hrs.	1 hrs.	3 hrs.
Av. no. of service hours/child	11 hrs.	8 hrs.	8 hrs.	9 hrs.	9 hrs.
TABLE 5.6 d					
Attendance and average hours per week use of pre-school childcare services by 0 - 5 year olds					
No service/attendance	9%	6%	9%	5%	7%
Nursery education	39%	6%	9%	37%	22%
	10 hrs.	4 hrs.	3 hrs.	10 hrs.	9 hrs.
Private day nursery	0%	5%	0%	0%	2%
	0	22 hrs.	0	0	26 hrs.
Registered childminder	6%	11%	9%	8%	8%
	11 hrs.	12 hrs.	19 hrs.	5 hrs.	12 hrs.
Creche	3%	18%	0%	0%	8%
	1 hr.	2 hrs.	0	0	2 hrs.
Playgroup	16%	56%	71%	34%	41%
	1 hr.	5 hrs.	5 hrs.	2 hrs.	5 hrs.
Mother & toddler group	50%	44%	29%	29%	43%
	2 hrs.	2 hrs.	2 hrs.	2 hrs.	2 hrs.
Nanny	1%	1%	0%	0%	☆
	40 hrs.	24 hrs.	0	0	32 hrs.
Unregistered paid minder	1%	0%	0%	0%	☆
	49 hrs.	0	0	0	49 hrs.
Other	11%	13%	16%	3%	11%
	4 hrs.	3 hrs.	1 hr.	1 hr.	3 hrs.
Av. no. of service hours/child	8 hrs.	7 hrs.	6 hrs.	6 hrs.	7 hrs.

	Buckie & Rathford Lennox	Donside	Gairloch Parish	Brae & Ollaberry	Average

TABLE 5.6 e

Number of different types and average hours of service attended by each child (0-12 months) per week					
No service/attendance	12%	23%	30%	50%	24%
One service	76%	69%	70%	50%	70%
Two services	12%	8%	0%	0%	6%
Av. service hours/child/week	2½ hrs.	3 hrs.	3 hrs.	2 hrs.	2½ hrs.

TABLE 5.6 f

Number of different types and average hours of service attended by each 1 year old child per week					
No service/attendance	26%	13%	33%	11%	21%
One service	65%	60%	66%	78%	66%
Two services	9%	27%	0%	11%	13%
Av. service hours/child/week	3 hrs.	5 hrs.	2 hrs.	4 hrs.	4 hrs.

TABLE 5.6 g

Number of different types and average hours of service attended by each 2 year old child per week					
No service/attendance	18%	7%	0%	0%	9%
One service	50%	53%	100%	62%	57%
Two services	32%	37%	0%	38%	32%
Three services	0%	3%	0%	0%	2%
Av. service hours/child/week	7 hrs.	7 hrs.	13* hrs.	4 hrs.	7 hrs.
			5* hrs.		

* One child with 40 hrs. provision per week, average for other 2 year olds in Gairloch is 5 hrs.

TABLE 5.6 h

Number of different types and average hours of service attended by each 3 year old child per week					
No service/attendance	-	-	-	-	-
One service	56%	53%	47%	83%	55%
Two services	41%	26%	35%	17%	32%
Three services	3%	21%	18%	-	13%
Av. service hours/child/week	6 hrs.	8 hrs.	7 hrs.	5 hrs.	7 hrs.

TABLE 5.6 i

Number of different types and average hours of service attended by each 4 year old child per week					
No service/attendance	1%	-	-	-	1%
One service	60%	35%	57%	84%	52%
Two services	30%	47%	29%	8%	35%
Three services	8%	18%	14%	8%	12%
Av. service hours/child/week	14 hrs.	9 hrs.	9 hrs.	11 hrs.	11 hrs.

	Buckie & Rathford Lennox	Donside	Gairloch Parish	Brae & Ollaberry	Average

TABLE 5.6 j

Number of different types and average hours of service attended by each 5 year old child per week					
No service/attendance	-	-	-	-	-
One service	80%	-	67%	-	60%
Two services	-	-	33%	100%	20%
Three services	20%	100%	-	-	20%
Av. service hours/child/week	11 hrs.	7 hrs.	6 hrs.	11 hrs.	9 hrs.

TABLE 5.6 k

Satisfaction with childcare facilities					
Satisfied	73%	42%	57%	65%	59%
Need more hours per week	11%	23%	11%	23%	16%
Not educational enough	5%	23%	3%	4%	11%
Difficult to get to - want nearer services	3%	12%	8%	19%	8%
Want better choice of local facilities	10%	19%	30%	0%	15%

TABLE 5.6 l

Weekly payment for childcare facilities					
No payment	2%	1%	3%	4%	2%
£1 - £2	83%	41%	48%	92%	64%
£3 - £5	6%	31%	22%	0%	16%
£6 - £10	2%	11%	14%	4%	7%
£11 - £20	3%	4%	0%	0%	3%
£21 - £40	3%	2%	8%	0%	3%
More than £41	1%	10%	5%	0%	5%

TABLE 5.6 m

Ideal service to complement existing childcare facilities & arrangements					
Satisfied with current	26%	13%	3%	21%	16%
Local nursery education	20%	52%	70%	16%	40%
More nursery ed. sessions/wk	5%	N/A	3%	5%	3%
Day nursery	20%	21%	38%	21%	22%
Workplace nursery	9%	4%	5%	21%	8%
Creche	21%	8%	14%	21%	15%
Local registered childminder	5%	6%	0%	5%	5%
Playgroup	13%	1%	5%	0%	6%

	Buckie & Rathford Lennox	Donside	Gairloch Parish	Brae & Ollaberry	Average
TABLE 5.6 n					
New services required					
No new services required	22%	11%	5%	26%	16%
Nursery education	21%	67%	54%	19%	42%
Day nursery	33%	40%	64%	19%	39%
Creche	21%	6%	3%	26%	15%
Playbus	14%	3%	3%	4%	10%
Registered childminder	5%	3%	13%	26%	7%
Playgroup	14%	3%	3%	4%	7%
Pre- and after-school care	14%	20%	10%	11%	15%
Holiday care scheme	23%	14%	18%	22%	19%
TABLE 5.6 o					
Transport to childcare facilities					
Always by car (own/friends)	58%	84%	75%	88%	73%
Sometimes by friends car	9%	22%	6%	8%	12%
Never by car (walk, bus, bike)	42%	16%	25%	12%	27%
Bus (sometimes or always)	1%	0%	0%	4%	1%
TABLE 5.6 p					
Satisfaction with transport to childcare facilities					
Satisfied	92%	81%	77%	87%	85%
Own transport imperative	5%	10%	23%	4%	8%
Distance & time too great	1%	12%	9%	8%	7%
TABLE 5.6 q					
Weekly travel cost to childcare facilities					
No cost	41%	2%	24%	8%	22%
£1 - £2	18%	40%	23%	25%	27%
£3 - £5	14%	18%	23%	8%	16%
£6 - £10	4%	9%	12%	8%	7%
£11 - £20	2%	5%	0%	9%	3%
More than £21	1%	0%	0%	0%	1%
Friend's car - not costed	2%	1%	3%	0%	2%
Own car - not costed	18%	25%	15%	42%	22%
TABLE 5.6 r					
Combined weekly childcare and travel costs					
Average for each area	£5.00	£12.00	£8.00	£4.00	£7.50

Chapter 6

SUMMARY AND CONCLUSION

SUMMARY

1. Changes in rural areas

The populations in all the areas surveyed were at a peak in the mid to late 19th century. In common with rural communities throughout Europe their populations then declined continuously. In 1971 this trend was reversed, and dramatic population increases (over 100%) were observed in Brae (Shetland), resulting directly from the oil related developments at Sullom Voe. Significant increases in population (20 - 40%) were recorded in Donside (Grampian Region), Gairloch (Highland Region) and Ollaberry (Shetland), and have been attributed to incoming families, rather than through growth in the indigenous populations. In Buckie & Rathford Lennox (Grampian Region) the population increased until 1981, but has subsequently declined.

1981 age structures of Buckie & Rathford Lennox and Gairloch were significantly more elderly than those recorded for Scotland, a common feature of areas which have undergone prolonged depopulation. In Donside age structures are similar to those of Scotland, while both Ollaberry & Brae, Shetland are comparatively youthful.

Historically, the survey areas have always had relatively high proportions of self-employed people in the work force and economies based on traditional primary sector industries such as agriculture, crofting and fishing. These industries have declined throughout the 20th century, accelerated by the development of the North Sea oil industry in the 1970's and more recently with the continued effects of European Community policies constraining fish catches and agricultural production. However, despite these changes, primary sector industries are still important to rural areas. The public and service sectors employ large proportions of the work forces, while tourism provides seasonal employment, particularly in Gairloch.

Male and female economic activity rates are high, and pluriactivity is common amongst those employed in the primary and service sectors. Women represent an increasing proportion of the rural work force, and the numbers of those with children aged under five are high - in three of the four areas studied - when compared to the 1988 GB average of 36% of women with children aged under five in full-time or part-time work (OPCS, 1990). Of mothers with pre-school children, 45% of those with children aged 3 - 5 were in employment, compared with 28% of mothers with children aged less than three. Similarly, 45% of mothers with only one pre-school child were in paid work compared with 23% of women with two or more pre-school children.

Survey data indicate that 19% of families with pre-school children in the study areas have weekly household incomes of less than £120. This is half of the 1988 Scottish average household income of £234 per week (Regional Trends number 25, 1990). In total of 34% of families have household incomes of less than £160 per week and 45% below £200 per week. There are clearly many families with pre-school children in rural areas who are living at unacceptable low levels of income, and some of whom are living in poverty. The average household incomes are highest in Donside, the area with the greatest number of incoming families. This suggests there are often significant differences in incomes between local and incoming families in rural areas.

Despite 19% of families having incomes of less than £120, 90% of all the families surveyed owned a car. This suggests that car ownership is correlated more strongly with remoteness than household prosperity. In turn the outlay on purchase, maintenance and running costs may well prejudice other aspects of quality of life.

Rural areas have experienced changes in household structure. Increased outward and inward migration has led to diminishing family support, particularly for incomers. Despite increasing rural populations, many 'new rural' families also feel isolated, lacking access to extended support networks. Falling fertility rates have lead to greater numbers of families with only one child who, isolated by geography, has few opportunities to socialise with others of the same age. There are also increasing proportions of single parent families, this survey identifying 7% overall, rising to 14% in one of the communities.

Changes in transport systems and their use are also a feature of rural areas. In general the quality of major roads have increased, but there continues to be a majority of minor single track roads. The improved major road networks have increased the numbers of families living in rural communities, but many of these commute to larger population centres for employment. Public transport has declined and is generally regarded as providing infrequent and inconvenient services. It is poorly used, with 85% of families in this survey reporting they rarely or never used the service. As mentioned previously, car ownership in rural communities is high despite lower than average household incomes. Ownership of one or more vehicles is essential for the majority of families who would otherwise be completely isolated through geography and lack of adequate public transport.

One of the communities surveyed, Gairloch, has many Gaelic traditions and a minority of Gaelic speakers. Until recently, the language has been under threat from increasing numbers of non-Gaelic speaking families migrating to the area, but it has now been recognised to be of great importance to the cultural identity of the area. The Gaelic language, although fragile, has been strengthened by the existence of a Gaelic playgroup, and the opening of Gaelic units at the local primary and secondary schools. Although current staffing is adequate, the development of these and any future childcare services have important implications for language training among childcare workers and teaching staff.

2. Current service provision

The current provision of childcare services differs greatly between the four communities surveyed, but in all cases there is less quantity of services and fewer opportunities for choice. Parents reported that although services are available, few are in their local neighbourhood, and so parents (usually mothers) have to be able and prepared to travel great distances with their pre-school children. Many childcare services are also oversubscribed.

In Buckie & Rathford Lennox, there are more full-time equivalent (FTE) nursery education places, per 1,000 of the population aged 3 - 4 (225), than in either in Grampian Region (136) or Scotland (170) as a whole. In contrast there are fewer FTE places with registered childminders per 1,000 of the 0 - 4 population, and there are no local authority or private day nurseries. Although mother & toddler groups are plentiful, there are few playgroups, all of which are oversubscribed.

Donside, the other community surveyed in Grampian Region, has no nursery education for pre-school children. In contrast there are a greater number of FTE places with registered childminders (50 per 1,000 of the 0 - 4 population) and at a private day nursery (25 per 1,000 0 - 4s). There are no local authority day nurseries. The large numbers of playgroups in the area compensate, but do not substitute adequately for the lack of nursery education.

In the Gairloch area there are fewer FTE nursery education places per 1,000 of the population aged 3 - 4 (69), than in either in Highland Region (119) or Scotland (170). There are also fewer FTE places available with registered childminders, and the area has no local authority or private day nurseries. Like Donside, the lack of nursery education in Gairloch means there are greater numbers of well attended playgroups.

It is not possible to calculate FTE places per 1,000 of the population aged 0 - 4 in Ollaberry & Brae, because the childcare services in these villages are used by children and families throughout the North Mainland of Shetland. Nursery education is widely available to children living in Brae, and also to those living further afield, if they are willing and able to travel distances of 15 or 20 miles each way. There are few other childcare services in the area, there being no registered childminders in Ollaberry and only two in Brae. There are no day nursery or creche facilities. The Ollaberry playgroup only meets once a week, while Brae mother & toddlers group meets on two occasions per week.

The local authorities in the survey areas did not run any sponsored childminding schemes offering support to children and families with any specialist needs. Neither are they providing any support networks or ongoing training for existing registered childminders.

The general lack of service provision for children aged less than five means there are few opportunities for children with special needs to participate in any integrated service. The specialist developmental playgroup in Buckie for children with physical disabilities, learning difficulties or emotional problems, reports that many children are able to progress to integrated nursery education. However, earlier options for integrated provision for children with special needs are not possible, because of the lack of quantity and range of childcare services, particularly for those aged less than three.

There are few childcare options currently available to school age children in any of the four communities surveyed. The only two identified were an after-school club operating in Buckie on Friday afternoons, and the private day nursery in Donside, which - while not currently running at full capacity - is willing to take school children in the afternoons and during the holidays. A minority of villages surveyed have operated holiday schemes in the past, but reported difficulty in recruiting staff. None of the villages were sure whether the schemes would be running again this summer.

3. Childcare arrangements

While making full use of the pre-school services available to them, the majority women report that these services are not meeting daycare requirements for either working or non-working women. Instead mothers tend to rely on informal arrangements with family or friends to provide daycare. While some women are satisfied, many dislike imposing on family and friends, and incoming families with few local networks and no family support find this difficult to organise.

Many mothers in employment work part-time and are often able to be home for their school age children. Those working in the afternoons usually also rely on family or parents of their children's friends to fill this temporary childcare gap. The after-school club in Buckie on Friday afternoons is used by children of some working parents. In Donside one other school age child is cared for after school by the private day nursery, and three other school age children (two in Donside and one in Gairloch) are cared for by registered childminders.

4. Use of service

267 families and 384 pre-school children in four communities were reached by the questionnaire survey. Of these only 27 children (7%) were not attending any form of pre-school provision, and all but one were in the 0 - 2 age group.

The most commonly used service is mother & toddler groups (43%, attended by 67 % of 0-2s and 27% of 3-5s) and playgroups (41%, attended by 11% of 0-2s and 61% of 3-5s). Although mother & toddler groups are traditionally for younger pre-school children, in some areas they are attended by children aged between 0 and 5, especially where there is no local playgroup (eg. Buckie). In some villages the small numbers of children mean that playgroups act as joint playgroup and mother & toddler groups (eg, Ollaberry, Shetland).

Nursery education is used by an average of 37% of the pre-school children aged between 3 and 5, but this ranged from only 10% - 15% of those in Donside and Gairloch, to 63% and 74% in Ollaberry & Brae, Shetland.

Registered childminders are used to care for 8% of children overall, and 8% sometimes used temporary creche facilities. The private day nursery in Alford, Donside is used by 5% of pre-school children in that area.

Although 36% of mothers of pre-school children are in either part-time or full-time employment, only 11% of all children are cared for by registered childminders, the private day nursery, nannies or unregistered minders. The childcare gap is usually filled by family or friends, but sometimes also by part-time nursery education.

All pre-school childcare services are well attended, with many playgroups and all nursery education classes having waiting lists. In all communities, but particularly Donside and Gairloch, parents take their children to several different playgroups each week in an attempt to compensate for having no access to local nursery education.

Over half the children only attended one form of provision each week (although this might comprise visits to two or more playgroups in different villages). However, many children, especially those aged 3 - 5, attended two or three different types of service each week. Despite the discontinuity in services and carers, mothers of children using several types of service considered their children to be able to cope well and adapt to these changes.

Playgroups and mother & toddler groups are commonly located in village halls or community centres, many of which are former primary schools. Some groups are able to use a spare classroom in their local primary school, and a minority rent privately owned halls. While premises were sometimes ideal, they are often only available part-time, are not always well heated, and frequently suffer from a lack of storage space. The number of sessions run by many local playgroups are also limited by the availability of premises in which they are held.

Although many villages had either a playgroup and/or a mother & toddler group, it is not uncommon for parents and children to travel several miles to attend. A significant proportion regularly travel 10 miles to and from each group. Parents are prepared to travel even greater distances for nursery education, with families in Strathdon (Donside) travelling 17 miles to Tarland (upper Deeside) and in Ollaberry travelling 15 miles daily to Brae. Some of the women using the private day nursery in Donside reported travelling several miles in the opposite direction to their work in order to use this facility.

Availability and location of registered childminders is considered a problem by women in all four communities surveyed. There are too few registered childminders, (eg, only one in the Gairloch area and none in Ollaberry), those registered are often not available to care for any more children, and are not always conveniently located for the women who wish to use them.

Playgroups usually charge fees between £1 - £2 per child per session, while mother & toddler groups often make a charge of around 50p - £1 per mother. In contrast parents of children in part-time nursery education (five 2¼ hour sessions) are only asked to contribute £1 - £2 per week towards snacks and drinks. The differential in charges mean that parents of children with no access to nursery education pay more per week to achieve the same number of hours of provision. In areas with nursery education, as many as 85% of families pay no more than £2 per week. In contrast, where there is no nursery education available, typical childcare costs ranged from £3 - 10 per week. Fees for registered childminders range from £1 up to £1.50 per hour. Charges at the private nursery in Donside are similar, but also relate to the parents' ability to pay. Overall 3% of families surveyed spend £21 - £40 each week on childcare, and a further 5% pay more than £41.

The majority of mothers and children (73%) always travel to childcare by car, compared to 25% who walk, 1% who cycle and 1% who use public transport. While satisfied with their mode of transport, many women commented that the time they spend travelling is too long compared to the short amount of time at the services. The majority of women estimate they spend between £2 - £10 per week transporting their pre-school children to and from childcare facilities, with 12% spending more than £11 each week. 24% of women surveyed travelled by car but did not cost this expense. A comparison of transport costs to weekly childcare costs, indicates that the parents in rural areas spend just as much, if not more, on transporting their pre-school childcare each week as they spend on the actual childcare facilities.

The combined average of weekly childcare and transport costs range from £4 - £5 per family in Shetland and Buckie & Rathford Lennox, to £8 in Gairloch and £12 in Donside. The average spending per family across the four survey areas is £7.50 per week. However, childcare costs can be as high as £60 for the use of a childminder for 40 hours per child per week in Donside. The differentials in spending between the survey areas result from both greater travel costs and more expensive childcare in Donside and Gairloch.

Several of the villages and communities surveyed have youth clubs or organised sports facilities for school aged children, but none have a daily out of school care service. Although Buckie has an after-school club, it only meets on Friday afternoons.

5. Demand and preferences for childcare services

The majority of women indicated that they would also like to have access to a greater range of services that would be: more flexible; available for more hours; and preferably local. This would enable parents to use the most appropriate services for their own and their children's needs. Current lack of choice often means pre-school children use local services whether or not they are appropriate. Registered childminders are also a scarce commodity in rural areas. Demand for services often outstrips the numbers of places available, with many playgroups and all nursery classes having waiting lists.

The women surveyed indicated that nursery education is the service they would most like access to for their pre-school children. There is also great demand (39%) for daycare facilities from both working and non-working mothers. 90% of these women said they would prefer a local authority day nursery, which they suggested should provide subsidised places thus enabling women to return to the work force without being penalised financially. Around 20% of women indicated they would find creche facilities useful, and 15% of working women would like a workplace nursery. Only 5% of women surveyed indicated that they would prefer to use a childminder than any of the other options.

Three out of four working and non-working mothers expressing a need for new childcare services indicated they would prefer these services to be at or near their homes. Only one in four suggested the service should ideally be at or near their place of work or training.

36% of mothers of pre-school children are currently in paid employment, but only 11% of all women use a childminder, day nursery or nanny to provide daycare. This means that two out of every three working women have to rely on temporary or informal arrangements, which many find unsatisfactory. 38% of the working mothers consider their current job to be at a lower level to the one they were in prior to the birth of their first child. The key reasons for this are: the lack of local, suitable and/or affordable childcare, and that the hours of their previous job were unsuitable.

61% of non-working mothers wish to join the labour market, and 17% would like to undertake some education or training at some time in the future . Lack of childcare is again considered to be a major barrier. Although many non-working women suggested a day nursery would assist them to carry out their future plans, most have resigned themselves to not returning to the labour market until after their children are at primary school.

The majority of women with school age children (71%) expressed the need for out of school care services. While many considered this would be useful in the afternoons, several working mothers suggested that pre-school care would be a useful addition. 10% of mothers of school age children indicated that, if available, they would use such a club every day, 35% during the holidays, and a further 51% would use the club occasionally.

6. Education and training

The majority of women with pre-school children responding to the survey generally have school or post-school qualifications. 83% have either O-grades or highers, and 53% have a post-school qualification. 26% of women had a college diploma or degree. In the communities with the highest proportion of incomers, there are also more women with post-school qualifications. This suggests that local women have not had the same opportunities to undertake education or training since leaving school.

At the time of the survey only two of the women (1%) considered education or training to be their main occupation. Although a minority of women are participating in part-time (usually vocational) community education courses, they did not identify themselves as undertaking education or training.

Overall 15% of women expressed a wish to undertake training or education in the future, but many doubted this would be possible, stating both the lack of local adult education opportunities, and of childcare facilities. One in four of the women also said that they lacked the necessary skills or qualifications to undertake this career change, suggesting many need encouragement, support and motivation to enable them to facilitate there future plans. Another research study of women returners in Ross & Cromarty District recorded high demands for training, particularly in information technology (Mann, 1991). Some of these women believed that refresher courses to update their existing skills would be essential before returning to the labour market.

CONCLUSION

1. Issues affecting childcare provision in rural areas

There are many issues which affect the arrangement of regular, good quality and reliable childcare to facilitate access to training or employment in rural areas. Some of these issues and other rural factors are summarised below:

- the scarcity of existing rural childcare;
- lack of innovative models for rural childcare;
- low density of under-fives population - small numbers of children over large geographic areas;
- declining birth rate projections for UK and Europe;
- the need for local provision to reflect the needs of children, parents and their local community;
- integrated facilities - providing equal opportunities for children with special needs;
- flexibility of care - with provision for working long and/or unsociable hours and weekends;
- costs of daycare - in comparison with lower wages earned by workers in rural areas;
- transport - both lack of access to private and public transport;
- the lack of suitable premises;
- the financial viability of childcare schemes for small numbers of children;
- the scale of demand - linked to low density rural population and the remoteness of rural firms;
- the size of rural firms, and employers attitudes to childcare;
- the need for special language provision and training for childcare workers in particular areas.

2. Policy options for developing childcare provision in rural areas

The numerous issues that need to be considered when developing rural childcare initiatives suggest that any schemes or models have to be flexible enough to incorporate these points and also to adapt to changing demands in rural areas. Requirements of parents must be assessed in conjunction with those of their children, and any childcare services must be assessed in context of their family's needs and in relation to community needs in general. These community needs may have a social and economic dimension and it is important that both should be taken into account. Community involvement in

H

the development of new facilities is important in ensuring that this wide range of interests is reflected, as well as services that reflect community experiences, values, and languages, thus contributing to the community's own sense of identity. Partnership approaches to the development of services now being tried in some areas are likely, for example, to require a more extensive local authority financial support than may be the case in some urban schemes.

Although this survey has shown that the demand for childcare from women in rural areas is high, the numbers of children involved may only be small and scattered throughout a wide area. These small numbers, compounded by declining birth rates, could affect the financial viability of rural childcare schemes.

Some European countries offer interesting models which are able to meet the varied demands of rural childcare. Some, for example, Hvepserenden in Sinding-Orre, Denmark (Appendix 2) offers a model which sustains the viability of schools where falling birthrates have dramatically reduced enrolments, by running childcare centres in them. Using school premises for such centres would also prevent the need for finding other or new purpose built premises

A multi-functional approach has much to offer in overcoming some of the problems of delivering services in rural areas. Multi-functional facilities may provide support and help to established pre-five activities, eg playgroups and mother & toddler groups, through providing access to facilities, information and possibly a toy library. They could offer services for pre-school children and older children, and a range of support services, resources for adults, and training opportunities at the same location. In addition to being more cost effective to run, such a facility would also enable women to gain confidence and refresh their skills prior to returning to the labour market. Age integrated centres for children (eg Denmark, Appendix 2) also offer more flexibility in terms of financial viability in rural areas.

An increase in daycare provision has implications both in relation to staffing and for increased training requirements of childcare staff and childminders. Although integrated training and childcare centres could provide support and ongoing training for these staff, it would be necessary to have some training input provided by relevant departments of local authorities. In some areas there will be a need for multi-lingual training for childcare workers, in order to develop and extend Gaelic childcare provision. Appendix 2 describes a two language training programme is provided for nursery workers in Friesland in the Netherlands.

Provision of daycare also has implications in relation to the type of premises required. Many premises currently used by pre-five groups are not either appropriate or available for extended use because of other demands on their time (eg church halls and many community centres). While it might be possible to run some daycare facilities from rural schools, new capital investment for multi-functional community facilities can be justified. Likewise, if any new community facilities are being developed in rural areas, they clearly should include facilities and accommodation for full-time daycare provision.

Childminders in rural areas receive little and sometimes no support from the statutory sector. Registration and monitoring is often undertaken by social work staff who might be based as far as 60 miles away (or three hours drive) on rural roads. The survey uncovered some evidence of unregistered childminders in rural areas, but this is not surprising because of the length of time taken for registration and because the women do not see any benefit in registration for themselves. A multi-functional centre could also offer a meeting place for registered childminders to meet and receive training, thus encouraging more women to undergo the registration process. An example of such a project in Averyron, France is listed in Appendix 2. None of the local authorities in the survey areas retain any sponsored childminders who could provide daycare for children with special needs or families experiencing difficulties. Such schemes often provide much needed respite for the child and family. The current levels of provision also make it difficult for local authorities to adequately fulfil their responsibilities to children in need.

There is a confused picture within local authorities as to which local authority departments have responsibilities for supporting pre-five services. Parents of children using these services are also confused at the numbers and roles of different departments. Although there is often planning between social work, education, and community education at a regional level, this does not always filter through to ground level. There needs to be a more integrated approach to planning for development of services at regional and local level and between the two levels. Planning should also include consultation with the prospective users of services and with the communities in which they are to be developed.

School age children can also benefit from increased facilities in rural areas. A multi-functional centre providing facilities for all the community could be used as a location of an out of school club. Again a curriculum could be developed to reflect local community experiences, values and languages.

The establishment of any new childcare and/or multi-functional community scheme has implications for funding. Costs can be shared or reduced by partnership or community business schemes, and in some rural parts of Scotland (see Appendix 3) there are also possibilities of funding from the European Structural Funds Programme. These provide an important new approach to the development of facilities in these areas, drawing together social and economic responsibilities for provision.

SELECTED INITIATIVES FROM GRAMPIAN, SHETLAND, AND HIGHLAND

1. The Upper Deeside Nursery Project, Grampian Region

The Upper Deeside Nursery Project, launched in August 1990, provides nursery education for children in their pre-school year living within the Aboyne Academy catchment area. The Academy has ten feeder primary schools from Torphins to Braemar, and six are currently being used as nursery bases. There are two nursery teams, each comprising a nursery teacher and a nursery nurse. Both teams have nine sessions of class contact time per week and visit the six nursery bases rotationally. The bases are Aboyne, Ballater, Braemar, Kincardine O'Neil, Tarland and Torphins. The head teacher of Tarland Primary School has also been appointed as the head teacher of the nursery project and assists with nursery teaching at Tarland.

During the development stage of the project there were consultations held with parents of pre-school children, local playgroups, the Scottish Pre-School Playgroup Association (SPPA) and teaching staff at the primary school in the catchment area. All were enthusiastic supporters of the project, and one of the key points to come out of these consultations is that nursery provision in rural areas must be flexible. There appears to be less pressure from parents in rural areas for five nursery education sessions per week (unlike urban areas). This is partly because of loyalty to local playgroups, but also because parents believe strongly that their pre-school children should continue to have contact with children with whom they will attend primary school.

The classrooms utilised by the nursery project are shared with the primary schools which use them for other other activities during the week (eg music rooms, or community rooms also shared by the local playgroup) and none of these would have been available full-time to set up a permanent nursery school on one site.

The flexibility of the project has meant that in the first year all 117 families who applied for nursery places for their pre-school children have been accommodated. This has been managed by providing for different numbers of classes and sessions at the six schools.

In the first year 1990/91, the provision was as follows:

Primary School	Number of classes	Number of sessions for each class
Aboyne	3	3 or 4
Ballater	1	1
Braemar	1	2
Kincardine O'Neil	1	2
Tarland	2	3
Torphins	2	2

Numbers in some classes are small and are sometimes combined together, for example, Aboyne classes 1 & 2 are combined on some days, while Aboyne classes 2 & 3 might work together on another. This flexibility has continued to give parents choice on the days and times of the sessions that their children attend. This gives greater flexibility, and, like all other aspects of the project, is constantly being reviewed.

The first year of the project appears to have been a great success with positive feedback from the children, parents and schools involved. There have been some practical problems with sharing classrooms and with storing and transporting equipment, but these have been resolved. The project aims to continue being flexible, and will draw up a different timetable each year dependent on the numbers of pre-school year children and demand for places in the Aboyne Academy catchment area. This might possibly mean that not all of the six nursery bases will necessarily be used every year if there is insufficient demand.

It is anticipated that the Upper Deeside Nursery Project will be adapted and replicated in other areas of rural Scotland.

2. Shetland Childcare Charter Group

This community childcare pressure group was established in 1989 to press for more services. Their 'Childcare Charter' argues that:

Parents should have a range of childcare provision to enable them to make the best choice for their children and their circumstances;

Children benefit from good quality, well organised and educational opportunities to play and learn with other children;

Childcare should be flexible to suit working and non-working parents, especially mothers. It should be convenient and at reasonable cost. Parents should be consulted about the development of local facilities, and have a say in running them.

The specific objectives of the Shetland Childcare Charter Group are that:

1. Every primary school should have a nursery class, catering for 3 - 5 year olds, by 1992;
2. Mother & toddler groups and pre-school playgroups should receive further council support and encouragement for their activities;
3. A day nursery should be set up in Lerwick offering full daycare facilities, particularly to assist working mothers. Demand in country areas should be assessed and small community nurseries, with appropriate funding and support, should also be set up;
4. Employers should be encouraged to set up workplace creche facilities and to sponsor holiday play schemes to assist working parents during school holidays;
5. The Shetland Islands Council should set an example by providing a day nursery for staff and a creche for members of the public with business in the council offices;
6. There should be consultation on the needs of working parents with school age children for after-school facilities and holiday playschemes;
7. The Shetland Islands Council should consult with parents, teachers, community and voluntary organisations, social services and other departments, in order to implement a programme to improve childcare in Shetland.

Since the Shetland Childcare Charter Group was established there have been some positive developments in pre-school provision: in 1990 Shetland Islands Council opened five nursery classes at four mainland primary schools providing a maximum of 200 pre-school children with the opportunity to attend five half-day nursery class sessions per week; both the Shetland Islands Council and Health Board have surveyed their own staff to assess their childcare needs; and in January 1991, 'Women in BP' established a working party to look into the demand for childcare facilities among the staff at the Sullom Voe oil terminal.

3. Play and Learning Sessions, Highland Region

Play and Learning Sessions (PALS) are an experiment in pre-school education supported by Education Committee of Highland Regional Council. There are 15 primary schools currently participating in Ross & Cromarty District, with a further six due to start in 1991/92. The experiment is being conducted in a variety of primary schools, both large and small, urban and rural, across a wide geographic area. One of these schools, Kinlochewe Primary, is in the Gairloch area.

PALS operates between February until the end of the summer term each year and encourages all children in their pre-school to visit the primary school for one or two play sessions per week. The scheme differs at each primary school, according to the space available and numbers of children participating. If there is a classroom available, parents (usually mothers) are able to attend with their children, but if there is little space and few children (as at Kinlochewe Primary), the children will join the reception or infant class.

Play sessions usually last between one and two hours and enable children to play with paints, water, sand, listen to a story and, if facilities allow, maybe also some cooking. An important element of the scheme is the distribution of pre-school packs to the children at the end of each play session. A typical pre-school pack might comprise two story books, a jigsaw, a lacing up game, beads, plasticine, a toy and maybe something to cut out and stick. The pack will be returned and exchanged the following week. The packs are designed not only to assist pre-school children develop increased hand to eye co-ordination, but also to encourage parents to play with and read to their children.

Where the scheme has been introduced it has been popular with pre-school children and their parents and also with teachers. Parents report that their children are less shy, mix and share more readily with others, and enjoy the activities they haven't participated in before. They believe the children benefit from the stimulation all the activities provide and also appreciate having access to a much wider range of toys and books. Teaching staff see PALS as an induction process for pre-school children. Not only do the children get to know the teachers and learn about the school environment, but the teaching staff are able to identify and note any possible difficulties or problems for the future.

While PALS is popular with those parents and children who are able to participate, there are some drawbacks with the scheme. Firstly, although schools attempt to choose a time that suits all parents (usually mothers), children of working parents, particularly those whose mothers work full-time, do not have the same opportunities to attend. Secondly, the scheme is very part-time, with only one or two play sessions available each week. Although widely praised, and the pre-school packs are a positive development, it is hoped that PALS will not become a cheap alternative to providing full-time nursery education to all pre-school year children, especially those living in rural areas.

4. West Coast Nursery Project, West Ross, Highland Region

This project was launched in August 1990 as an experiment in peripatetic nursery education provision in rural areas. The project employs a part-time nursery teacher who runs a nursery class in four different primary schools once a week. The schools are in Aultbea, Inverasdale and Poolewe (in Gairloch Parish) and Badcaul (to the west). There are, in theory, up to ten nursery places available at each of the four schools, and all pre-school year children in these villages attend. In 1990/91 the actual numbers of pre-school children attending each class are as follows:

Primary School	Number of nursery class places	Number of pre-school children in each class
Aultbea	10	12*
Badcaul	10	5
Inverasdale	10	5
		(3 Poolewe & 2 Inverasdale)
Poolewe	10	6
		(4 Poolewe & 2 Inverasdale)

* Nursery teacher requires additional support, provided by local playgroup leader.

There have been problems with accommodation for the nursery classes. Badcaul Primary is the only one of the four schools with a classroom available for the nursery class. In Aultbea the class meets in the village hall, which is not considered ideal as the class does not have strong enough links with the primary school or teachers. The Inverasdale and Poolewe nursery classes meet in infant classrooms with primary 1 - 3 pupils. At these two schools P1 and nursery pupils have participate in experimental play and activity based learning together. While this has been successful in the first year of the project because current P1 pupils had no nursery education, alternative arrangements are likely to be made in successive years. Much equipment is transported from school to school each day, while large pieces of equipment are rotated every four weeks. Storage of additional equipment has and continues to present problems.

Although parents have been enthusiastic about the development of the project and pre-school children enjoy attending nursery classes and find them stimulating, nursery education provision is so part-time that it tends to cause a lack of continuity. The project aims to remain flexible and will adapt in the future in response to changing numbers of pre-school children.

SELECTED INITIATIVES FROM EUROPEAN COMMUNITY COUNTRIES

BELGIUM

Theux: Centre Wallon D'Animation et de Co-operation

The centre has been involved for a number of years in a range of initiatives in the region including the establishment of agricultural fruit and beef co-operatives and the development of services. The centre has carried out a review of care and education needs of families with children in the area and this has led to a number of projects, including the establishment of a nursery which is heavily over-subscribed, the examination of the possibility of a project for the establishment of a nursery in an industrial zone in the region, and the training of staff for the nursery.

Action research on rural childcare needs

Province of Luxembourg - Districts of Dinant and Philippeville.

Project undertaken by Office de la Naissance et de l'Enfance (ONE) with Femmes Prevoyantes Socialists (FPS). Action research project examining rural childcare needs in six communes. Findings of the study include:

* lack of adequate structure of services particularly for children under three and school-age children;
* lack of choice;
* constraints on women's employment;
* high, sometimes exorbitant, cost of private provision despite staff not necessarily being qualified;
* grandparents used for care do not necessarily have appropriate skills or desire to take care of the children.

The study suggested the need for a collaborative approach between professionals and action at the different levels of the family neighbourhood and community. This is seen as a return to traditional childcare patterns and the aim is to achieve this as through development of parent committees and wider community involvement including the voluntary work of old and young people. Parent committees and associations have at the same time sought public support not only in the form of finance but in the establishment of a supportive framework. Initiatives which have been undertaken include the establishment of a centre for children from 0-12 years, a community nursery, two "homework" schools and a "midday" school care service.

Kakelbont, Bovenbergstraat

Small rural centre in Flemish community providing variety of services including nursery, occasional care for children under three, outside school hours care for children under 6, support for childminders and a number of other services. Adjacent to nursery school and primary school. Accommodates 10-12 children aged 0-6 and is funded by the local authority.

DENMARK

Municipality of Ringkøbing: Hover Børnehus

An age integrated rural daycare centre

The initiative was taken by a group of parents, all residents of Hover, a rural parish of some 550 inhabitants, including approx. 73 children aged up to 10. The work of the group was primarily aimed at:

* ⋆ strengthening the parish, the school and the life of the local community

The group carried out a survey of the demand, which showed that:
* ⋆ parents were looking for a flexible childcare scheme. Many of them work part-time or flexible hours, and were having to pay for - and occupy - more hours of childcare than they required.
* ⋆ some form of after-school leisure facilities would be needed in the next few years.

The group identified the need for flexible daycare arrangements to meet the needs of the rural area, proposed that the teacher's tied accommodation in Hover be used, being centrally located and providing the possibility of utilising the facilities of the school.

The centre

Hover Børnehus was established as an age-integrated daycare centre, as provided for in Section 70 of the Danish Social Assistance Act (pooling arrangement).

Ringkøbing Municipality contributed approximately 250.000 kroner towards the refurbishment of the tied house and in addition, according to a co-operation agreement, a fixed grant was given towards the running of the centre, based on the number of children enrolled.

Hover Børnehus currently offers about 16 full-time places at a cost to Ringkøbing Municipality of approx. 23.000 kroner per place per annum. This corresponds to 65% of budgeted costs and is based on the Municipality's average cost per place for similar age groups. The cost is thus fixed along the lines of normal daycare centres.

Hover Børnehus offers modules of 10, 20, 30, 40, and 50 hours per week, matched by corresponding pro rata payments. The centre currently has 32 children, some of whom are part-time, others full-time. A full-time place costs the same as a corresponding Municipal place, which currently costs approx. 1.178 kroner. The flexibility arrangement thus results in a lower price per place per child, since the children would otherwise have occupied a full-time place.

The grant from the Municipality, if calculated proportionally, is based on the equivalent of full-time children; e.g. 5 children enrolled for 10 hours attract the same grant as one full-time child. The parents and staff jointly agree on the timing of the enrolled hours, which demands a great deal of flexibility on the part of the staff. The discontinuance of the 10-hour module has been considered, as it makes heavy demands on resources.

Hover Børnehus is governed by the parents; a board hires and fires staff and takes virtually all decision concernings the centre. The centre employs professionally qualified staff. Ringkøbing Municipality acts as consultant to the centre, i.e. it provides assistance according to the wishes of the parents. For the time being, it will also underwrite any deficit.

The centre constitutes a facility for the local community which to a large extent makes use of the resources already available, such as the older generation, the farming environment, etc.

Furthermore, Hover Børnehus has a very high degree of parental involvement, not least because the parents have worked very hard to set up this facility; consequently feeling that the centre belongs to them.

The Municipality of Herning: Hvepsereden Sinding-Orre

An age integrated daycare centre on school premises

The school in Sinding was threatened with closure due to falling school rolls. Children of non-school age were in private daycare. Some children attended centres outside the local area.

A working party comprising childminders, parents, school governors, teachers and a citizen's group was set up to put forward proposals for the solution of the problem of childare. Its proposals were submitted to the education authority and social service department of Herning Municipality. A scheme was approved for a period of two years, starting on January 1 1988. On January 1 1990, "Hvepsereden" was made permanent.

The centre

The age-integrated daycare facility was set up as a self-governing body, as provided in Section 69 of the Danish Social Assistance Act, and located on school premises. (A class was moved into a recently acquired pavilion to make room for the daycare facility, thus enabling close contact between the school and the centre). The children are aged from 3 to 13 years, and the centre is open for 52½ hours a week. The scheme meets the care requirements of 10 children in private daycare, 25-30 children aged 3-13 in children's day institutions, and 15-20 playschool children. There are 30 full-time places shared between 65 children, including approx. 10 children in the care of private childminders. 4 modules of equal size are offered: full-time, ¾, ½ and ¼ places. The parents can choose the numbers of hours per day they want their children to attend, with the staff making arrangements accordingly.

The Nursery Head Teacher and Deputy Head Teacher supervise 3 daycare centres, arranging inspections, home visits, payroll administration etc. "Hvepsereden" is used as a guest daycentre in case of illness, holidays and the like, as well as offering playschool facilities one morning a week for children in the care of private childminders. There is an "ordinary" playschool facility twice weekly for children being looked after at home.

Staff numbers correspond to that of other day care centres in Herning Municipality, based on the number of full-time places. Staff costs are approx. 2.500 kroner per child per month.

The concept "all our children - all our experiences" is the basis for very close co-operation and many activities. The presence of "Hvepsereden" at the school has, for example, led to the parents building a playground on the school lawns, which is open to the whole neighbourhood outside school hours. The staff's break periods coincide with the play periods of the school, and the teachers' staff room has been opened to all staff. The Head of the centre is responsible for the educational aspects of "Hvepsereden", but from the beginning regular meetings have been held between her and the Principle of the school.

A report on the creation of "Hvepsereden" and its educational work has been prepared.

FRANCE

Olemp Nursery/Halte-Garderie★, Aveyron

Location

The service, for young children under six years of age, operates in the commune of Olemps which has 3000 inhabitants. It has a rapidly expanding population with an increasing number of working women.

Structure

12 childminders provide care for 38 children in their own homes. The service operates from Monday to Saturday (inclusive) all year round. The Director, an infant teacher, is employed for 17 hours per week. She manages the service and organises personnel recruitment.

The service is only available for children where both parents are working. It operates on a regular, but frequently part-time, basis.

Amenities

The service and each childminder is organised by the Conseil General of the local community.

Funding

Costs forecast for 1991 = 150 Francs per day per child (I day = 8 hours)

Staff costs - 90% of expenditure
Contribution from families - 44% of income
Contribution from Caisse D'Allocation Familiale - 44% of income
Contribution from commune of Olemps - 4% of income (of which 50% is for lease and 50% is a grant).

Activities

Every Thursday afternoon (2.30.pm to 6.00.pm) the children attend a local centre accompanied by their childminders. The centre is equipped with games, toys and materials which provide them with collective and personal developmental experiences. The group setting also allows the childminders to meet one another and share and exchange work experiences, and is organised by the Director who is available to all parents at this time.

L'Esperou Nursery/Halte-Garderie★, Gard

Location

The service is situated in the small village of L'Esperou in Cevannes at the foot of Mount Aigoual, 95 Km. from Nimes.

The village is geographically isolated with widespread habitation and a number of small hamlets. There are difficulties of communication in the winter. The area has a late school entry (5 years) and is administratively tied to a more important village in the valley (Valleraugue).

Organisation

The service operates with a parental structure. It is managed by parents with the help of a nursery council composed of user parents, administrative parents, and staff and is elected locally.

Amenities

There are 14 places in the nursery (as per regulations) and 2 places in the halte-garderie★ with one infant teacher and a child welfare auxiliary.

Funding

Equipment: 50% General Council
                40% CAF (Caisse D'Allocation Familiale)
                10% DASS

Fees:
                300 Francs/month/family
                80 Francs/day for local residents
                100 francs/day for "foreigners" (tourists)

Local services (heating and lighting) are organised by the local council and funding of other services by the CAF.

Activities

The service gives priority to pre-school activities in collaboration with the (single class) village school, and work on language with an orthophonist. Tourists' children are accepted in the short and long vacations. The nursery therefore serves (in its location and with its usual personnel) as a non-residential leisure centre which balances its annual budget and contributes to the vitalisation of a rural area in difficulty and where tourism is a trump card in its economic dynamics.

★Halte-garderie provide part-time/irregular care for children aged 0-6. They are generally open 8-9 hours per day.

GERMANY

Rural Kindergartens Project

The project covers 29 kindergartens in three Bundeslander: Bayern, Baden-Wurttenberg and Wiederbachen, and is run by Deutsches Jugendinstitut (DJI) in co-operation with Deutscher Caritasverband, the umbrella organisation for Catholic kindergardens in West Germany. The objectives of the project are:

    a. to analyse the situation of kindergartens in different rural areas;

    b. to assess living conditions of families with children aged three to six using the kindergarten facilities;

    c. to assist in helping the institutions to meet the needs of parents and children in rural communities.

The project has examined the history, culture and social structure of each village, the impact of structural change in the rural areas on the socialisation of children and the situation of families; socio-pedagogical work in the kindergartens; relevant legislation; and social policy for children in rural communities.

Families

Selected interim findings from a survey of all families participating in the rural kindergartens include:

* Farming families are a minority within the villages. Only 11% of children's parents are involved in agriculture.
* Labour force participation among mothers is high, with 11% working on the farm, 7% in the family enterprise and 30% as employees/clerks.
* 66% of the fathers and 53% of the employed mothers commute to work outside the village.
* 14% of the children in the kindergartens are in a one child family; 51% have one sibling; 25% have two siblings.
* The number of children varies with the working situation of the families, with farmer families having the most children. 62% of farming families had three or more children. Half of the full-time employed mothers have one child; 34% have two children and 15% have three children. Half of the part-time employed mothers have two children; 26% have one child and 17% have three children.
* Extended family structures are diminishing in rural areas: only 15% of the children were growing up in families with relatives other than mother and father.
* 5% of the children are living in one parent families.

> *"It's the newcomers you usually find in the mother and child groups. The old ones don't need the groups so much because they've got their families to help them - grandmothers, aunts and sisters and their larger families on the farms. But it's different for the newcomers . . . in our case our nearest aunts live 500 miles away. My mother is 79 and she lives in Schleswig Holstein. So if we ever want to go out we always need a babysitter."*
> *(Housewife and mother of two and new to the area)*

> *"The relatives all live up in Mannheim. But I'm really quite happy about it. I'm forever hearing from mothers whose parents are living with them and their children - there are sometimes some pretty big problems when they interfere. So I'm really quite happy that my folks are far away. Life is really good and I can still call on someone - that older lady - if I need help. I have peace and quiet and can bring up my children my own way without having a mother-in-law at my back telling me to do things differently."*
> *(Mother of two with a part-time job and new to the area)*

Kindergarten provision

Hours of opening in kindergartens vary with three principal variations in the institutions studied.

a. Opening hours in the morning and afternoon (from 7.30 to 11.30/12.00 and again from 13.30 to 16.30).

b. Opening hours only in the morning (7.30 to 11.30/12.00).

c. A proportion of kindergartens responding to demands for daycare through extended opening hours.

d. Demand for places in rural kindergartens exceeds the availability of places and one result of this is that the number of children at the age of three decreases. Only 15% at this age attend a rural kindergarten.

e. The opening hours available failed to match parents working hours:
48% of parents with both a full time job and commuting require further daycare provision.

Interim conclusions

Social changes in the rural areas of Germany involve an increasing variety of family structures and lifestyles. The number of farmer families has diminished and many rural areas are attracting the workers from the city who wish to provide their children with a better environment. Provision for children in rural communities is not meeting the needs of families either in levels of services or in offering services which take account of the daily routines of families with young children. a possible area of development lies in the development of kindergartens as neighbourhood centres able to respond in a more flexible way in meeting specific needs of families in the community and offering play facilities which are adequate to the change in living conditions and forms of socialisation within rural areas.

(Extract from unpublished paper prepared by Irene Berger for European Childcare Network Seminar "The Childcare Needs of Rural Families", Athens, April 1990).

GREECE

Summary of Family Survey carried out in the Prefecture of Thesprotia in the Region of Filiates

Thesprotia is one of the seven most underprivileged rural areas in Greece. In the post-war period poor living conditions and lack of infrastructure together with the impact of the civil war have contributed to heavy outmigration in this and many other rural areas in Greece. However, many of those who move into urban areas maintain close relationships with their villages, often retaining their property and visiting frequently, and in some areas keeping their voting rights in their birth towns and villages. Agricultural and development problems include:

* small size of agricultural holdings
* bureaucracy and centralisation in the public sector contributing to lack of information and low uptake of development funds
* poor social conditions and infrastructure including lack of asphalted road network, electricity and water supply systems and sewage systems, inadequate medical facilities and lack of educational and cultural facilities.

Population

There is considerable variation between winter and summer months with the population increased by 73% in the summer months. The age and gender structure also changes significantly from winter to summer. Women form 61% of the population in the winter but only 52% in the summer; people over 40 constitute 62% of the population in winter but only 44% in the summer.

Educational attainment

Illiteracy (defined as being unable to read or write) is non-existent for the under-40 age group; 5% of men and 8% of women over 70 are not able to read or write. The general level of education attainment is low, and lower for women than for men.

Transport

Of the twenty-six villages in the study only half were connected with asphalted road and there were only two where the houses were connected by marked roads.

Households

Households size increases significantly in the summer months with 70% of households having four or more members in the summer compared with 54% in the winter months. Although 98% of households had access to electricity only 9% were connected to any water supply, 80% had lavatories (outside the house), less than half had a bath/shower.

The number of extended families is still extensive but nevertheless a minority of all families.

A large number of fathers worked away from the area. 35% of husbands with four or more children and 22% of those with three were absent for periods longer than six months compared with 4% of those with one child.

Table 1: Household structures

No. of families	Extended families	Nuclear families	One-parent families
747	342	313	92

Employment

62% of women were in paid employment, 41% in agricultural and livestock, 19% in home handicraft and 2% in service industries. Of mothers with children under 10, only 10% were economically inactive. 34% were involved in agriculture and livestock, 21% home handicrafts and 35% assisted their spouse.

Education

14 of the 26 villages have a primary school but there is only one teacher in each school which is required for all classes. A significant proportion of all children have to travel more than half an hour to school. Educational performance of pupils is in general low.

Health

None of the villages have a medical centre. 20 villages have access to a doctor, one to a nurse and five have no medical provision at all. 8% of mothers received no medical attention during pregnancy.

Childcare

Table 2: Childcare arrangements

Childcare of mothers working outside the home	
Mothers bring along the child	29%
Grandparents	27%
Brothers/sisters	32%
Neighbours	9%
Relatives	3%
Nursery school	0%

Children's social and cultural activities

Of 141 children surveyed the most common activity that children took part in was sport. 104 of the 141 children took part in sporting activities. Only 20 participated in groups such as Scouts, etc. and only one had ever visited a cinema or theatre. 69 assisted in their parents jobs, most commonly as shepherds and goat herders, etc.

Parental attitudes to nursery education

The survey found considerable gender differences in attitudes towards nursery education with twice as many women as men in favour.

Perception of impact of lack of facilities on children

The survey found that the overwhelming majority (77%) of parents thought that living in the village was adversely affecting their childrens' career.

(Extract from paper prepared by Vivie Papadimitriou for the European Childcare Network Seminar, "The Childcare Needs of Rural Families", Athens, April 1990.)

LUXEMBOURG

Rural Childcare in Luxembourg

In common with the rest of the Community, levels of provision are substantially lower in the rural regions of Luxembourg. Only 8% of the available services are located in the rural areas where care by relatives remains the most common form of childcare.

Social, economic, and demographic changes have focused attention on the requirements in rural areas. These changes include:

* Population shift from urban to rural areas. In the four departments of Capellen, Mersch, Remich and Grevenmacher the number of children aged 0-4 has increased by between 10-13% while the child population in this age group has been decreasing in the city of Luxembourg and the industrial region of Esch-sur-Alzette.
* Female activity rates in the rural areas have increased significantly by more than the average increase in the country as a whole.
* Changes in household structures with fewer extended families within the same household.

The Luxembourg government have announced a national programme for developing childcare provision adapted to the needs of a rural environment. This focuses principally on provision for disadvantaged regions and groups including farmers and their spouses.

(Extract from unpublished paper by Jean Altmann)

NETHERLANDS

Friesland: Two Language Training for Nursery Workers

In Friesland, in the north of the country, Fries is officially recognised as a second language. Professional training centres now offer students a two language programme.

The expansion in childcare facilities over recent years has created a shortage of childcare workers in rural as well as urban areas.

PORTUGAL

Rural Childcare in Portugal

Portugal is a country of extensive rural areas with substantial educational and economic requirements in relation to provision. 62% of women with a child under 10 were employed in 1988, the second highest level in the community and a further 6% were unemployed. Only 10% of employed women with a child under 10 had part-time jobs. Women are extensively involved in agriculture but are less likely to be involved in off-farm economic activity; in many areas fewer employment opportunities, cultural norms, and more formal childcare requirements than in on-farm work deter off-farm employment. Problems in the delivery of services in rural areas include the scattered and declining population, low car ownership and poor roads. This has led to the examination of a number of itinerant programmes and more informal systems involving volunteers and parents themselves. A number of programmes have explored provision from a wider community perspective and, more specifically, examined the needs of rural women and their role in rural development.

Centro de Animacao Infantil de Campo-Valongo
(Children Animation Centre of Campo Valongo)

This semi-rural area has an economic base of agriculture, craft and textiles. The centre began in 1979 as part of a wider project covering 12 villages; this particular centre continues with limited financial assistance. The project involved the training of volunteers "animators" to stimulate development of facilities using local people to help build centres, and old people to help as informal teachers. The centre has 50 children aged 3-5 and three staff - comprising 2 local "animators" and 1 early childhood teacher. The project worked with women as well as children, establishing an association, Women for Tomorrow, and developing literacy, health, and information programmes. The centre currently lacks the funding to extend its hours to meet care requirements of parents or even to give adequate renumeration to its current staff, and would like to be able to provide vocational training.

Projecto ECO, Educacao De Infancia Itinerante S. Bras De Alportel Algarve
(Itinerant pre-school programme for isolated children - funded by Van Leer Foundation)

S. Bras De Alportel is a hilly area to the north of Faro with some 10,000 inhabitants. The district's economy is largely based on cork production, agriculture (including olives and almonds) and service industries including tourism. Cultivation of land is difficult contributing to outmigration from the area. The small town which gives the district its name - S. Bras de Alportel has two primary schools, one nursery school, and one combined nursery school/day nursery, the latter providing for children from 3 months-5 years, (Portuguese children start school at six). There are eight other primary schools in the district but no other pre-school provision. Roads are poor and only around a quarter of the rural population have access to transport- usually a van or truck for the transport of produce. The council operates a minibus once a week to take people to the doctor, bank, shops etc. The programme was developed as a means of giving children in the year prior to their starting school some pre-school experience with a parental involvement programme. Two trained nursery teachers work with 29 families, the furthest family living 15 kilometres from the town. The teachers visit the families for one hour a week and the child visits the nursery school for 3 times in the year and is taken on outings. Some sessions are arranged with several families. Activities take the form of the development of two projects in the year - one undertaken by all the children on the common theme of animals (reflecting the agricultural base of the area); the other based on the child's own interests.

The programme is in its final year of funding from Van Leer and is currently being evaluated. The project has highlighted the absence of pre-school provision and is thought to have provided parents with insights into the education which their children are receiving when they start school. The teachers comment on generational difference in attitudes towards education - grandmothers account for around a quarter of family members they work with in the programme. The relationship between teachers, parents and grandparents and between children from the group sessions were felt to have been very valuable. However, the project also highlighted the wider needs of families and in particular the need to offer more opportunities for the mothers, currently felt to be often very isolated and economically marginalised in a district with few associations for women. 15% of the mothers worked outside the home generally as maids and shop assistants and it is thought that more of the mothers would want to undertake employment if more opportunities were available. The project co-ordinator supported by the local council, is now to undertake a survey of the needs of families.

EUROPEAN STRUCTURAL FUNDS AND CHILDCARE

The European Community's structural funds comprising the European Regional Development Fund (ERDF), the European Social Fund (ESF) and the European Agricultural Guidance and Guarantee Fund, Guidance Section (EAGGF) were reformed in 1988 in order to ensure that the closer integration of Member States resulting from the Single European Act is accompanied by balanced social and economic development. The Fund objectives have been clarified and prioritised, giving more assistance to less developed regions and improving the co-ordination of the funds. The budget has been substantially increased and in 1993 will reach 14 billion ECUs - doubling the real value 1987.

The Fund's Objectives

The Funds have five major objectives. These are:
1. Promoting the development and structural adjustment of less developed regions.
2. Converting the regions seriously affected by industrial decline.
3. Combating long term unemployment.
4. Encouraging the integration of young people into employment.
5. a: Speeding up the adjustment of agricultural structures.
   b: Promoting the development of rural areas.

The Areas They Cover

Three of the priority objectives are geographically restricted in scope. Within the United Kingdom, only Northern Ireland is covered by Objective One. In Scotland, some areas seriously affected by industrial decline are covered by Objective 2. All areas are covered by Objectives 3 and 4. Some rural areas are covered by Objective 5b.

How Childcare Fits In

Work carried out for the European Commission by the Commission's Childcare Network (1) established that inadequacies in childcare contribute to a number of significant structural inequalities within the European Community.

Inadequate Childcare:
* affects women's access to employment, education and training.
* affects hours of work and nature of employment

* reinforces gender divisions in labour through assumptions about male and female work.
* contributes to skill shortages
* increases employers' recruitment and training costs

It has now been recognised that the development of childcare facilities can assist and stimulate economic development:-
* through removing barriers to the effective use of the potential labour force
* through facilitating entry to training in areas of required skills.

Childcare Conditions Attached To Funds

Since October 1989 a new clause has been introduced to Community Support frameworks. This stipulates:

"The actions and measures taken in the framework of this Community Support framework must conform with and, where appropriate, contribute to the impact of community policy and legislation relating to equality of opportunity between women and men. In particular, consideration must be given to training and infrastructure requirements which facilitate labour force participation by people with children."

Funding Possibilities in Relation to Particular Objectives

1. Development of Nurseries and Out of School Schemes which enhance the economic potential, development or structural adjustment of areas. Childcare facilities, health and education facilities contributing to structural adjustment. (Establishment and running costs for limited period) - Objective 1.
2. Nurseries incorporated within industrial sites or business centres servicing small and medium sized enterprises (SME's). (Establishment and running costs for limited period) - Objectives 1 and 2.
3. Provision facilitating training in areas where women are substantially under-represented, training and occupational reintegration for women returners, maximising local employment development potential and measures for young people requiring vocational training. Innovatory projects and actions accompanying measures to support those providing access for training.(Financing of places or allowances) - All Areas.
4. Provision facilitating diversification of the rural economy (Establishment and running costs for limited period) - Objective 5b.

The Distribution of Funds

The management of the allocation of funds is through partnership at local, national, regional and community level. Member States submit development plans setting out their proposals for achieving the five objectives of the fund, complemented by more detailed operational programmes. These indicate the measures which will be carried out aimed at resolving specific employment problems and having to demonstrate clear links with plans and priority activities set out in the capital's community support frameworks. All individual projects have to form part of an operational programme. In the UK, programmes are structured on an organisation type basis and are compiled at the appropriate national or regional level.

Objective 2 - Areas in Scotland
Travel to work areas:–

Eastern - Alloa, Falkirk, Stirling, Kirkcaldy, Dunfermline, Bathgate, Arbroath, Dundee.

Western - Glasgow, Lanarkshire, Greenock, Cumnock & Sanquhar, Kilmarnock, Irvine, Dumbarton, Ayr, Girvan.

Objective 5b - Areas in Scotland
Travel to work areas:–

Highland and Islands - Badenock and Strathspey, Campbeltown, Dunoon and Bute, Elgin (part), Forres, Keith (part), Invergordon and Dingwall, Inverness, Islay/Mid-Argyll, Lochaber, Oban, Orkney, Shetland, Skye/Western Ross, Sutherland, Thurso, Western Isles, Wick, the intermediate areas of Dumfries and Galloway (this means that the whole of the Highland and Islands Regions are included).

Community Initiatives

5% of the European Fund is set aside for special programmes. The programme of proposal relevant to childcare is the NOW Programme (All areas).

Within the framework of the measures provided by the NOW initiative, the Commission will support:

(a) The provision (fixtures and equipment) of childcare facilities especially in zones of industrial concentration for the benefit of enterprises, of groups of enterprises or vocational training centres;

(b) operating costs of childcare facilities related to vocational training centres;

(c) vocational training for childcare workers, to raise both the quality of the services as well as the conditions of employment of the staff concerned.

The infrastructure aid will be limited to objective 1 areas. Preference will be given to measures combining infrastructure creation as well as vocational training.

Cohen 'Structural Funding and Childcare: Current Funding Applications and Policy Implications' CEC V/2267/89-EN

Structural Fuding Factsheet (Number 5) Scottish Child and Family Alliance

Other relevant programmes are:–

LEADER

Liaison between actions for the development of the rural economy involving establishment of local rural development groups in regions covered by Objectives 1 and 5b.

LEDA

Local Employment Development Action Programme

EUROFORM

Programme to promote new occupational qualifications, new skills and new employment opportunities.

MIRIAM

Model scheme for information on rural development initiatives and agricultural markets.

BIBLIOGRAPHY

Arkleton Trust (1991) "Rural Policy and Deprivation in Europe: From Analysis to Action". Report of the Arkleton Trust Seminar, Tarland, Aberdeenshire 1990 (Forthcoming).

Benfield, G. (1990) "Rural Deprivation and Community Work", Occasional Paper No. 12, Community Development Foundation.

Bennett, W. and Laxton, M. (1988) "Practice and Organisational Issues in Rural Social Work - a discussion paper", (Unpublished Scottish Office Paper).

Cohen, B. (1990) "Caring for Children: The 1990 Report", Family Policy Studies Centre.

Cohen, B. (1989) "Structural Funding in Childcare: Current Funding Applications and Policy Implications", Commission of the European Communities, V/2267/18-EN.

Mann, L. (1991) "Women Returners to the Labour Market in Ross and Cromarty", Ross and Cromarty District Council, February 1991.

Midwinter, A. and Monaghan, C. (1990) "The Measurement and Analysis of Rural Deprivation", Department of Government, University of Strathclyde, (Report prepared for COSLA, February 1990).

Oppenheim, C. (1990) "Poverty: The Facts", Child Poverty Action Group 1990.

Scott, G. (1989) "Families Under Five in Strathclyde", Glasgow College, 1989.

"Area Profile - Ross and Cromarty" (1990) HIDB.

"Area Profile - Shetland" (1990) HIDB.

"Area Profile of West Ross - Statistical Area 6" (1983) (Confidential Report) HIDB.

"Childcare Needs of Rural Families" (1990) Commission of the European Communities, V/1732/90 - EN.

"General Household Survey 1988" (No. 19), OPCS, HMSO (London) 1990.

"North Mainland Local Plan - 1989", Shetland Islands Council Planning Department.

"Regional Trends 1990" (No. 25), Central Statistical Office, HMSO (London) 1990.

SED Statistical Bulletin No 15/AZ/1990 "Provision for Pre-School Children", 1990, Scottish Office.

"Training and Enterprise: Priorities for Action 1990/91" Labour Market Assessment Grampian and Tayside Area, The Training Agency, Scotland 1990.

Women in Europe, "Childcare in Europe 1985-1990", Commission of the European Communities, 1990.

Printed by HMSO Edinburgh Press
Dd 0287458 C20 7/91 (289151)